Syrian Hamsters or Golden Hamsters as Pets

THE COMPLETE OWNER'S GUIDE –
TOLD FROM THE PERSPECTIVE OF A CURIOUS
SYRIAN HAMSTER CALLED "LITTLE FELLA"

Little Fella, Karola Brecht, Mich Medvedoff

Official Website: www.syrian-hamsters.com

Storie di Karola – Waltraud Karola Brecht
Nussloch, Germany

Storie di Karola – Internet Marketing Business
Waltraud Karola Brecht
Siedlerstr. 11
Nussloch, Germany 69226
www.storie-di-karola.com

Book Layout ©2013 BookDesignTemplates.com

Ordering Information:
Quantity sales. Special discounts are available on quantity purchases by corporations, associations, and others. For details, contact Karola Brecht at the address above.

Syrian Hamsters or Golden Hamsters as Pets/ Karola Brecht. —1st ed.
ISBN 978-3-944701-00-4

CONTENTS

[1]Introduction 3

[2]Little Fella's Family Tree 5

   1) Meet the Hamster 5

   2) Ewww... Are Hamsters Really Rodents? 7

   3) Where are Syrian Hamsters From? 9

   4) Meet my Cousins 11

   5) Hamster Biology 17

[3]Are you Hamster Material? 19

   1) Is a Syrian Hamster a Good Pet for Me? 19

   2) Circadian Rhythms and Funky Sleeping Hours ... 21

   3) Life is Short 23

   4) What'll it Cost Me? 23

   6) Summary of Monthly Upkeep-Costs 24

[4]Hamster Hunting 25

   1) Golden Syrian Hamsters for Sale! 25

   2) Pick a Ham, any Ham 32

   3) Male or Female? And determining "he" or "she" ... 33

4) How to Select a Healthy Specimen 38

[5]Hamster Supplies 41

1) From Cages to Condos, Hamster Real Estate 41

2) Hamster Bedding 46

3) Food Bowl and Water Bottle 46

4) Hamster Enrichment.. 46

[6]Make Room for your New Roommate........................ 49

1) Hams Prefer Privacy.. 49

2) Ideal Temperature 50

3) Is your Home Hamster-Proof?............................... 50

4) Syrian Hamster Names 51

[7]What's on the Menu? 53

1) Hamster Nutrition 53

2) Hamster H2O 58

3) Treats? (Yes, Please!) 58

4) Dear, Diary: Bottomless Cheek Pouches 60

[8]Hamster Hobbies... 63

1) Fitness Junkies 63

2) Setting up the Home Gym 64

3) Hobbies and Other Distractions.................................64

4) Quick Note on Children.................................65

[9]Hamster on the Loose! 67

1) Hamster Houdinis.................................67

2) How to Bring him Back?.................................70

[10]Nitty Gritty: Syrian Hamster Care.................................73

1) Hamster Bathroom.................................73

2) Cleaning-out Syrian Hamster Cages 74

3) Tips to Reduce Odors 78

[11]Inside the Hamster Mind 83

1) Discern Body Behavior.................................83

2) Problem Behavior.................................89

3) Taming and Training.................................93

[12]Recognizing a Sick Hamster.................................97

1) Recognize a Sick Hamster 97

2) Hamster Illnesses.................................98

3) Clipping your Hamster's Nails and Teeth 102

4) Hibernation.................................103

5) Facts of Life, Getting Older 103

6) Dear, Diary: My Very Bad Hair Day 104

[13] Hamster Breeding 107

1) Raising a Hamster Brood 107

2) It Takes Two 108

3) Birthing Process and What Next? 109

[14] Websites for Syrian Hamsters 111

1) U.K. Relevant Websites 112

2) U.S. Relevant Websites 112

Index 113

Photo Credits 114

ABOUT THE PUBLISHER 117

Dedicated to all those who believe humans and hamsters can live peacefully together.

Not dedicated to: snakes, cats, dogs, and any other domestic animal that mistakes hamsters for food. Which is the most ridiculous of notions. Hamsters are for loving and cuddling, not eating!

About the Author

Little Fella is a writer for "Hamster Stories," the first hamster-only journal that circulates in over 100,000 hamster habitats around the World. Mr. Fella has covered the Westminster Hamster Show for HAMY and National Public Radio for the past two years.

His forthcoming book of inspiration and motivation, "Think Outside the Cage" is scheduled to release this Fall. Mr. Fella lives with a menagerie of four humans: Mom, Dad, Stevie, and Katie in Berlin Germany. There is also a snake named Edith living in the same household; however, Little Fella doesn't see much of her (fortunately).

[1]

Introduction

If there is a perfect pet, hamsters are it; or they at least come pretty darn close. With their twinkling eyes, plump bodies, and dexterous feet, no wonder hamsters have amused children and adults with their cute antics for generations.

Before purchasing a pet hamster, one must take into account various considerations. Are you introducing a Syrian hamster into your home so that your child may learn the joy and responsibility caring for a pet may bring? Or, perhaps you're in the market for an adorable companion for yourself?

Less likely, but still possible, are opening a traveling animal circus and have been told hamsters are excellent performers (they are)? Whatever your reasons, consider this book your hamster Bible.

Whether you are simply toying with the idea of hamster-ownership or already have a furry buddy in your home; the Authors have compiled well-researched information and personal experience to create a comprehensive book on everything hamster related.

This book is unique. And we're not just saying that to sell copies. Told from the perspective of both human and hamster. The hamster-authored sections comprise the bulk of the book, penned by Little Fella (a three-year old Syrian Hamster). Mr. Fella draws from his immense knowledge of hamsters (after all, he is one!) to present a refreshing reference guide.

So curl up in that easy chair - or your hamster ball - and enter the World of the Hamster!

Little Fella's Family Tree

1) MEET THE HAMSTER

You may be surprised to read a reference book about pet hamsters written by an actual hamster. Initially, the publisher of this book was incredulous that I, Mr. Fella, member of the rodent family, might pen a book for humans, or as I prefer to call: "furless giants." However, it came down to money (as most things in your human world). My co-authors of this work pitched the project to the publisher, citing: "why should us humans write a book about hamsters, when we can just hire an actual hamster to write it for us?"

As I said, the publisher only warmed up to the idea after they realized they could hire a hamster for cheap. After all, what good is money to us hamsters?

Go ahead. Ask me. How much did I make off this very important piece of hamster literature?

.................?

Okay, give up? I'll tell you: 2,000 hamster treats and a lifetime supply of mealworms. If you've eaten mealworms, you will agree that I made out like a bandit!

Well anyway, I guess I'll get on with it. The burning questions you've wondered your entire life but were too embarrassed to ask: Hamsters. What are they? Where do they come from? Do they make good "pets" (or the phrase I prefer is "roomie")? And do they eat anything besides mealworms?

This book will answer these questions and more, but first, allow me to clear up the most basic of questions, "What are Hamsters?"

2) Ewww... Are Hamsters Really Rodents?

My hamster family, which includes: Mom, Dad, Omelet (sister), and Jambon (brother). We're commonly known as "Syrian hamsters," or "Golden Hamsters." To scholars and other smarty-pants, we're known as Mesocricetus auratus.

Mesocricetus auratus kind of sounds like the name of a dinosaur, doesn't it? You can call me Mesocricetus auratus if you really want to, but most hamsters (and humans) call me Little Fella! I was born at Claws and Paws pet shop. It's a fun little pet store, maybe you've heard of it?

At Claws and Paws, I was among dozens of baby hamsters ready to go to human homes. However, in the wild, hamsters are considered vulnerable due to habitat destruction from humans meddling with our natural environment.

To get revenge, we've upped our cuteness factor and have now invaded your homes under the guise as "pets." Muhahahaha!

All kidding aside, thanks to the furless-giants out there that do adopt us hamsters and welcome us in their homes, our species is not only preserved, we're proliferating!

My Mom used to joke that I should count my lucky stars. She said being born a hamster in the 21st Century is the Golden Age for us Golden Hamsters.

Living in human homes, we're basically born into an early retirement. Living as pets, our needs are met (as opposed to living in the wild, we'd need to forage during the day). Our domestic lives are full of eating, burrowing, and exercising.

Life's sweet. Maybe it's not a coincidence that furless-giants enjoy having us hamsters around so much. After all, both hamsters and furless-giants are mammals. As such, we share more similarities than we think!

Hamsters belong to the rodent family, which includes: mice, rats, guinea pigs, chipmunks, squirrels, beavers – even porcupines! And we rodents have you furless-giants outnumbered.

Did you know over 40% of the World's mammal populations are rodents? Scary, huh! Do you feel surrounded or what?

3) WHERE ARE SYRIAN HAMSTERS FROM?

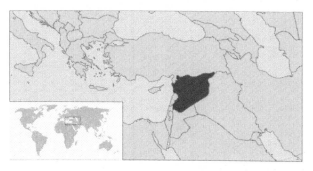

I come from a long line of burrowers. My Father was a burrower. My Grandfather was a burrower. My Great-Great Grandfather was a burrower.

In the wild, Syrian hamsters dig burrows up to 10 feet deep. This has a lot to do with the climate in our native Syria. Syria is a country that is very hot during the day, and considerably cooler at night.

We're also an awfully secretive bunch – furless-giants don't really know when hamsters first distinguished themselves as a species within the rodent family, with our burrows being so deep and hidden. The earliest known description of Golden, or "Syrian" Hamsters was recorded in 1797 by Alexander Russell.

Alexander Russel was a physician living in Syria and came across what he considered an unusual specimen. (Now this next part makes my stomach turn, the idea of Dr. Russell dissecting an innocent member of my species, but here goes).

Russell was intrigued by the deceased hamster's pouch on either side of his mouth. Upon dissecting the pouches, Russell noted:

> *"...the pouch on each side of the hamster's mouth was stuffed with young French beans, arranged lengthways so exactly and close to each other, that it appeared strange by what mechanism it had been effected; for the membrane which forms the pouch, though muscular, is thin and the most expert fingers could not have packed the beans in more regular order. When they were laid loosely on the table, they formed a heap three times the bulk of the animals body..."*

Three times the bulk of an animal's body weight is impressive, however I've pouched even larger amounts of food, myself. So. Meh.

Anyway, the surprising thing about Russell is he did not lay claim to discovering this new species of hamster; instead, he mistakenly classified the Syrian hamster under the "Common European Hamster" nomer.

Ooops! There is nothing common about us Syrian hamsters. You missed out, Dr. Russell. You could have called my variety of hamster (a very special variety of hamster) the A. Russell hamster. Ah, well.

It wasn't until 1839 that British zoologist George Robert Waterhouse stumbled upon my ancestors and proclaimed discovery of a new species: Syrian hamster. (Of course, we existed for thousands of years before that – but furless-giants are funny that way)

INTERESTING FACT: DID YOU KNOW THAT THE WORD "HAMSTER" MEANS "MR. SADDLEBAGS" IN ARABIC? ALTHOUGH I'VE NEVER BEEN TO SYRIA MY NAME DERIVES FROM SYRIA. FUNNY, DON'T YOU THINK?

OK, so how did the wild Golden Hamster get from the deep burrows in Syria to that hamster ball rolling around on your carpet? (Again turns my stomach a little)...

In the late 1920s, Saul Alder, a parasitologist at the Hebrew University of Jerusalem was conducting research on disease. He chose to study an adult female wild Syrian Golden hamster and her brood. Due to reasons I'd rather not get into – the adult female was set loose. Some of the babies were taken back to the lab – and later, introduced to British and US pet markets in the 1940s.

4) Meet my Cousins

I have a lot of cousins. Some are crazier than others. There's hundreds of species of Hamster. Most live in the wild, some haven't even been discovered by furless-giants yet!

Five Types of Domestic Hamsters:

- Me (Golden or Syrian Hamster). Syrians also include Teddy Bear Golden, or Black Bear Hamsters
- Chinese Hamster
- Dwarf Russian Hamster

- Campbell Hamster
- Roborovski Hamster

These are the five basic varieties of hamsters you will find in the pet store – with Syrians being the most popular (well, that goes without saying).

INTERESTING FACT: DID YOU KNOW THAT NEW VARIETIES OF HAMSTERS ARE BEING CREATED ALL THE TIME? THE RUMOR IN THE HAMSTER WHEEL IS THERE ARE HAMSTER BREEDERS OUT THERE THAT BREED HAMSTERS BASED ON COAT COLOR AND LENGTH FOR A VARIETY OF NEW HAMSTER LOOKS AND STYLES. NEW HAMSTER FASHION IS ALWAYS TRENDY

Furless-giants aren't the most organized lot. With many of these hamster varieties known by common names as well. For example, there are many different Syrian Hamster types. Some come in short coats and others in long, fuzzy coats. The long, fuzzy coated guys are called Golden Teddy Bear hamsters. Teddy Bear hamsters have the same temperament as shorthaired Syrians, unless of course you're talking about my Uncle, a Teddy Bear Hamster named "Wilbur." He was a Teddy – nothing cute and cuddly about that ham. Used to make me run 10 miles in my hamster wheel when he paid a visit. Ugh, always dreaded a visit from curly-haired Wilbur.

Another nuance are Winter White and Campbell hamsters – both are sometimes called Djungarian Hamsters. They're from a region in Siberia called Djungaria.

Allow me to get really professorial with you and explain in detail the characteristics of each species. I learned all this in hamster school – got an A in the class so I know what I'm talking about. So listen up!

SYRIAN GOLD HAMSTER

The crème de la crème of pet hamsters - and that's not just my opinion!

Syrians measure 15 to 17 centimeters (6 to 7 inches) and weigh 141 to 198 grams (5 to 7 ounces). In the wild, Syrian coats are usually golden brown with a white belly and chest. However, thanks to breeders' twisted imaginations: they've introduced 20 color variations. Variance in coat color is called a morph.

Colors, or "morphs" include: black, cinnamon, violet, yellow, grey and come in short-haired and long-haired coats. As previously mentioned, Syrian hamsters with long-haired coats are known as Teddy Bear hamsters. Now, if their coat is a golden color then they're called "Golden Teddy Bear." Syrian hamsters live longer than all other known species of hamsters. Plus, we're the most social of all breeds when it comes to furless-giants. My mother always taught me to be polite and friendly with furless-giants.

With hamsters on the other hand, we're something else... You know that movie "Rocky"? Haven't seen it?
You should really check it out – anyway, when it comes to Syrians and other hamsters... we fight like the Italian Stallion. Our fighting instinct usually doesn't kick in until we reach 5 weeks old. But hey, how many 5 week olds do you know that can box?

Okay, you may want to skip these next few pages because this is the part where I talk about hamsters other than us, Syrians.

If you do decide to continue reading, you'll come to discover the fact that Syrian hamsters are ham-stars, while other hamsters are just, you know... Rodents. (editor's note: although it's true all hamsters belong to the rodent family, non-Syrian hamsters are just as interesting as Syrian hamsters, contrary to what Little Fella would like you to believe).

CHINESE HAMSTER

Certainly the "mousiest" looking of hamsters, the Chinese hamster's body proportions as compared with other hamsters appear long and thin with a relatively long tail. Their temperaments can be on the testy side when getting to know you, but once tame are some of the most gentle and calm hams I know. However, California and New Jersey regard these hamsters as pests and require a special permit to own them.

CAMPBELL HAMSTERS

Campbells were discovered in Mongolia by W.C. Campbell in 1902. (Wow, that guy must have been mighty proud of himself to give the newly discovered hamster his name).

Campbells measure in the range of 7.6 to 10 centimeters (3 to 4 inches) and are generally grey in color. These hamsters actually like living with other hamsters.

Weird, huh? They're small and dainty – like little dumplings, or so I'm told. The males are heavily involved in the birthing process – helping females raise their young. (They don't box, so what else are they gonna do?)

WINTER WHITE / DWARF WINTER WHITE RUSSIAN HAMSTERS

Winter White hamsters, or Dwarf Winter White Russians (jeesh, that's a pouch-full, ain't it)? Also referred to as Siberian or Djungarian hamsters.

Winter Whites don't actually remain white; they're coats change color with each passing season. In the winter, they are bright white but in the summer, they change to a grey color with a black stripe down their side. However, these color coat changes generally occur in the wild. You might see some of this color seasonality if your hamster is exposed to more natural light year-round, as that's what influences these coat changes.

Why are they called dwarfs? Well, because they can be teeny tiny, as small as 5 to 10 centimeters (2 to 4 inches). Don't let their size fool you: if you have any allergies to dander, dust, or pet hair – beware as these little guys are more likely than any other hamster breed to cause allergic reactions.

They're awfully cute though! They remind me of a little rabbit with their floppy ears. The expression on their face is always perky. But again, don't be fooled by their small size or cuteness. They are slow to bond with furless- giants and may get nippy if they don't feel comfortable with you.

ROBOROVSKI HAMSTERS

Very quick and equally timid, these tiny guys are considered a "look but don't touch" pet. Super skittish with furless-giants, these aren't the most interactive of hamsters. One must observe rather than play, per se. And even to view these critters proves a challenge as regular light bothers their sensitive eyes. It is recommended to view them under a red light (which they cannot see).

5) Hamster Biology

The distinguishing feature of mammals is they nurse they're young. Humans nurse. Whales nurse. And Hamsters nurse.

Likewise, all species within the rodent family share common features as well. One obvious feature that springs to mind is the buck-toothed grin of rodents – from my Aunt Gertrude to your neighborhood chipmunk.

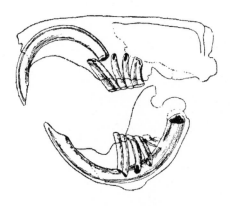

Rodents have two long sharp teeth called incisors on both the upper and lower jaw. These teeth are worn down by constant chewing throughout the rodent's life. Fortunately, the incisors continue to grow. Can you imagine if they didn't? How would my Grandpa Scruffy ever chew a nut again? Grandma Scruffy would have to chew the nut with her incisors into little pieces and feed them to Grandpa. Gross...

Another neat feature in our teeth is a gap between our incisors and molars called a diastema. This gap provides space to store food or even debris such as wood and straw for building burrows. It's also a neat hiding spot if you want to tease your siblings and hide their breakfast.

And finally, a major characteristic of us rodents is our ability to birth young at early ages. Imagine having a baby when you were 2 weeks old? Sounds strange to you, but perfectly normal for us rodents.

Why are rodents so biologically prolific? For thousands of years rodents lived in the wild alongside many predators like owls and eagles. To keep the family tree going, us rodents had to find a way to multiply and prosper – and that meant reaching sexual maturation early. Additionally, rodents give birth to a large litter (a dozen or more pups); further ensuring the survival of the species.

Aside from all of the above what makes rodents alike? We're a-dooooor-aaaaa-ble. Who can deny our tails, cheek pouches, and chubby bodies? Sure, mice and rats have a bad rap with homeowners, but you must admire their solid work ethic!

[3]

Are you Hamster Material?

1) Is a Syrian Hamster a Good Pet for Me?

Furless-giants ask this question all the time, and to be honest – I'm getting a little tired of it. The question you should instead ask is: "Am I a good fit for a hamster?"

After all, hamsters cannot simply unlock their cage and walk out the door like you guys can.

All hamster breeds, including us Syrian Golden hamsters are sensitive types.

You've got to understand we're small little creatures that evolved to live in warm, climates deep underground.

These environments tended to be quite stable. When the weather was too hot or too cold, we would simple hibernate our days away until the climate improved. Before falling in love with the idea of a pet Syrian hamster, consider the following golden hamster care:

TEMPERATURE

Syrian hamsters are from the desert. As such we've evolved to live in stable, warm environments. If the temperature drops below 5C (40F) then we go to sleep for a long time – maybe forever.

LIGHT

Hamsters are sensitive to bright light. As we're most comfortable underground for hours of the day, too much natural sunlight gives us the worst sunburn. In that sense, we're kind of like rodent vampires. Except we don't want to suck your blood or anything...

TINY LUNGS

Did you know our lungs are the size of a postage stamp? We require clean, fresh air circulating in our miniature lungs. So that probably rules out all potential hamster owners in the city of Los Angeles (unless you happen to be a rich movie-star with an awesome three tiered burrow system deluxe hamster condo).

STABILITY

Hamsters do not tolerate changes in their environment very well. A move might be stressful for a furless giant; but for a hamster it's downright traumatic, making us anxious and possibly even ill.

If you foresee any moves in the near future.

Or even house remodeling where the hamster habitat must be moved from one room to another, consider another pet – I hear goldfish are nice. Or an ant farm.

TRAVEL MUCH?

If you are a frequent traveler and plan to have various friends look after your hamster, then we may not be a good fit. Again, this follows under "stability."

Hamsters can grow very attached to their furless-giants. If you're out of the house all the time, you will be missed. Don't expect us to constantly get comfortable with different furless-giants who stop by for five minutes to dole out our food rations. We are monogamous and will not bond on your whim every time you go on "business" to Las Vegas.

Outside of these limitations, hamsters can adapt to almost any situation. If your lifestyle is relatively stable, if you have a dedicated space for your hamster that won't be moved much, and if your home is clean, quiet, and comfortable than we have a deal. Got it? Good.

2) CIRCADIAN RHYTHMS AND FUNKY SLEEPING HOURS

As far as humans are concerned, us Hamsters may be the noisy neighbors in the cage next door.

I sleep during the day. It's not that I'm lazy or anything, it's just my nature. While you're busy at school and work – we are deep asleep in our burrow...

Just when you've brushed your teeth and climb into bed for the night? That's when we wake up and come out to play!
We're the "party animals" of the rodent world.

When my furless-giant, Stevie, complains to his parents that he doesn't want to go to bed but it's past his bedtime, I wonder "what's the big deal? I'm just now having breakfast. Why not let the kid stay up?"

If you wish you could stay up as late as you wanted and sleep in through your alarm clock in the morning, then maybe you should have been born a hamster!

In the wild, my Great Great Uncle Pernisious Fellow lived a simple life. Hermetic life. He would sleep in the deepest part of his burrow of hay or dirt to avoid nocturnal predators, such as owls (who are the most ferocious of beasts, be careful if you ever see one). After sunset he would forage for food for a couple of hours, then return to his burrow at dark. My Uncle lived this way for many years.

And hamsters today carry on that tradition. It's just how we're designed. So if you're a light sleeper, and the sound of a midnight run on our exercise wheel will wake you up, than a hamster pet may not be the best choice for you.

We have a strict regime for looking young and fit at any age.

My Mother and Father taught me the trick to looking a young 36 weeks throughout your life is to stick to a schedule. To get an idea of a day in the life of a Syrian hamster, please find a typical day's itinerary:

1. Up at 6PM.
2. Exercise in the wheel o'fun or hamster pull-ups on the bars of our cage. We're from the desert and like to break a nice sweat.
3. Breakfast
4. Salt lick
5. Tidy the burrow
6. Time for bodily grooming
7. And finally, scent marking (more on this later)
8. Lights out at 6 AM

Little Fella

As you can see, hamsters busy themselves throughout the night and prepare for sleep just as you are getting up for school or work.
If you think you might not be able to accommodate your hamster's natural schedule, consider another pet.

3) LIFE IS SHORT

In furless-giant years, a hamster lives for just two –four years. Four years to us hamsters is the ripe old age of 75 in your years. So don't cry over it!

However, it may be difficult for furless-giants and their young to say goodbye to a cherished hamster that has passed on. Be sure to take very good care of your hamster while they are alive. Follow the instructions in this book for feeding, cleaning the habitat, and ensure your hamster receives plenty of exercise. This will help your furry friend live to a natural age. Of course, if you and your hamster are lucky maybe he will live beyond four years old, in which case he might be a candidate for the Guinness Book of World Records!

4) WHAT'LL IT COST ME?

Hamsters are not only loveable, we're also thrifty roomies! The low initial set-up costs, as compared to a cat or dog are very attractive. The initial and long-term costs below represent a range of prices from major pet supply retailers. You can comparison shop on the Internet from the many sites available (see chapter 14 for U.K. and U.S. web sites).

5) SUMMARY OF INITIAL SET-UP COSTS:

Aquarium/Cage: minimum 45 L, or 1858 cm2 (10-gallon, or 2 square feet) £25 to £50* ($40 to $75). I really recommend a high rise cage with the option to plug on a 10-gallon aquarium. It makes sure that we hamsters have enough room for feeling happy!

Visit the official site of this book to get more detailed information: **http://www.syrian-hamsters.com**

Food Bowl: £2 to £3* ($3 to $4)

Water Bottle: £4 to £5* ($6 to $8)

Litter/bedding: £6 to £9* ($9 to $14)

Food: £3 to £6* per 1 kilogram ($4.50 to $9 per 2 pounds)

Chew treats: £2 to £3* ($3 to $4)

Toys: £3 to £5* ($4.50 to $6.50) each

Hideaway/den: £5 to £6* ($6.50 to $7.50) each

Tunnel: £3 to £4* ($4.50 to $5.50) each

Exercise Wheel: £7 to £8* ($12 to $13) each

Nesting Material: £3 to £5* ($4 to $6.50)

Total Initial Cost: **£54 to £74*** ($82 to $102)

*costs in $ may vary due to currency fluctuations

6) Summary of Monthly Upkeep-Costs

Litter/bedding: £12 to £18* ($18 to $28)

Food: £3 to £6* per 1 kilogram ($4.50 to $9 per 2 pounds)

Total Monthly Cost: **£15 to £24*** ($22.50 to $37.50)

[4]

Hamster Hunting

1) Golden Syrian Hamsters for Sale!

How often – if ever – are you able to choose a member of your family? Usually you are born into a family with no choice in the matter. When it comes to pets, you do get to choose a member of your family. However, humans wrongly consider they are the ones choosing the pet when visiting the pet store or breeder; however, more often it's us hamsters that choose You!

Through our behavior, whether we act shy and scared, friendly or cuddly; we display a demeanor to draw interest or repel potential owner.

The question is, will YOU be able to decipher our communiqué? In this chapter, your author, Moi, will provide you with the gossipy details on how to notice the pet that noticed you first! Whether you shop at the local gargantuan Pets R Us Center, or a breeder.

Now that you've decided you want to bring a hamster into your life, your next step is to find one. If you've chosen to bring a Syrian hamster home, you'll be happy to learn you can conveniently find us at your local pet store or breeder – and that a trip to Syria is not required.

Consider what purpose is your hamster pet: is it simply for you and your child to enjoy and observe? Or do you have hopes to play hamster matchmaker and breed hamster babies?

Where you fall on this spectrum determines what source to locate your hamster friend and the price expected to pay.

PET SHOPS

Unfortunately pet shops have a bad rap, often offering pups and felines from abusive "puppy mills." However, because hamsters have been blessed by extreme fertility and breed so very often, you can rest assured insensitive breeders do not find the need to cut corners and institute abusive puppy mill practices for the sake of raising baby hamsters.

When shopping at a pet store, recognize these clues:

- Cages for Syrian hamsters might as well be boxing rings. Do not purchase from a shop that group Syrian hamsters in the same cage. Unless the pet store is starting a professional hamster boxing circuit, the hamsters are likely anxious and disturbed, having lived within unnatural proximity to other adult hamsters.
- Look for well cared for hamsters. Only purchase hamsters that are clean and look well cared for. Overcrowded or un-sanitary conditions make for sad, unsociable hamsters that are more susceptible to disease.
- Knowledgeable staff? Does staff respond intelligently to your questions? If they do, likely the hamsters have been in good hands. If they don't, then you must question if the hamsters were neglected or mistreated due to ignorance.

How can you tell if the staff is knowledgeable on the hamster sub-ject? Pretend you're Alex Trebeck and put the staff on the panel at Jeopardy with various questions, such as: "Are the hamsters male or female?" "What is the breed of the hamster?" and "How old is the hamster?" If the sales associate offers you assured replies than they likely know what they're talking about. I will also give you the nitty gritty tips in this book so you will have the answers for yourself.

- Hamsters are not to be sold in bulk. Hamsters are not to be sold like a tub of peanut butter at your local discount super store. If the pet shop is offering a two for one deal, or if the hamsters are sold at bargain prices, walk away... very quick-ly. These are warning signs the hamsters may be old, un-dernourished, sick, or all three. Choose another hamster joint for your hamster needs.

BREEDERS

If you are thinking about choosing a hamster with higher pedigree, or if you plan to breed or show hamsters, then consider purchasing from a breeder.

You can find Syrian hamsters for sale from breeders, as well as many other hamster varieties. There are many advantages to purchasing from a breeder. These folks have intimate knowledge of the hamster, including their family history. Breeders have likely spent more time individually with each hamster than at a pet store, and invested in the personal care and socialization of the hamster, better equipping the little guy with the tools to bond with your family more readily.

You will have closer supervision from a breeder, with the opportunity to ask questions and learn valuable information. Plus, if you're interested in breeding or showing hamsters yourself, what better way to break into the community than to purchase from a breeder.

Of course one downside with breeders is prices may be slightly higher than pet stores. This shouldn't deter you as the quality and care invested in each animal most likely exceeds what you would find at a pet store. Where to find breeders?
Hamster breeders are everywhere. Your neighbor, or even that old lady who loves to wear purple across the street may be a hamster breeder. One really never knows!
If the breeders are in hiding and refuse to reveal their identities to you, there are other sources; whether you live in the United States or the United Kingdom.

IN THE UNITED STATES:

The Internet Hamster Association of North America
(http://www.ihana.us/) provides a wealth of information on hamster ownership as well as a breeder directory. To add to your comfort, the Association requires their breeders to subscribe to a
breeder code of ethics.

IN THE UNITED KINGDOM:

Although no longer active, the British Hamster Association has a
map on their website with breeder details. Simply search for a
breeder near to your location
(http://www.britishhamsterassociation.org.uk/locate_breeder.php).

Established in 1949, the National Hamster Council is the oldest such
institution. With a small membership fee, you have access to a
monthly newsletter, upcoming show information, and an online
database of active breeders in the United Kingdom
(http://www.hamsters-uk.org/).

CLASSIFIEDS

Of course hamsters do not live long by furless creature standards,
but there may be individuals who lost interest and need to hand
their hamster over to another owner. Check out classifieds for particularly great deals. However, you cannot be sure of the level of
care placed upon the hamster during their tenure with said owner.
Use your eyes and discern the hamster behavior to determine
health and well being to stave off unexpected issues that may come
up.

Also consider the age of the hamster – elderly hammies have great stories to tell (except for the long, Golden Hamster Sagas my Grandfather tells...) remember: the more mature hamsters will have less time getting adjusted to you – and less time to build a bond.

On the positive side, you may be able to score not only a hamster from the owner – but all the hamster necessities (cage, wheel toys, etc). Unless of course the owner likes to play with the hamster accessories himself...

NOTE: ALTHOUGH IT IS POSSIBLE TO PURCHASE HAMSTERS ONLINE, WE CANNOT RECOMMEND IT! HAMSTERS ARE VERY SENSITIVE CREATURES, NOT A MAIL PARCEL. WHEN CHOOSING HAMSTERS ONLINE, ENSURE YOU CAN VISIT WITH THE OWNER (AND HAMSTER) PRIOR TO MAKING THE PURCHASE. THANK YOU.

"I love running cross country... On a track, I feel like a hamster."

-Robin Williams (famous actor)

HUMANE SOCIETY

Finally, some hamsters are unfortunately abandoned by their owners due to a move or disinterest; or perhaps hamsters born with a defect and are unwanted. Consider shopping at the local humane society – or even your local animal rescue operation.

SCHOOL

Have a kid in school? Ask their teach if the classroom hamster is in need of a home stay during the summer term. This is a particularly great way to see how serious your child is about hamsters – you might even consider it a trial run before taking the hamster-ownership plunge.

GET HANDS-ON

Above all, when choosing your hamster, ensure the seller allows you to hold the hamster first. Just tell the clerk, "I Want to Hold your Ham!" (Singing is not required).

Holding the ham allows you to get a sense of the hamster's personality. Hold him gently and stroke his head and belly. We love this!

If the hamster responds and acts inquisitive – maybe you found your new buddy. Holding the hamster also gives you an opportunity to examine the health of the ham (more on this at the end of the chapter).

If the hamster is anything but cuddly: shy, nervous, anxious, timid... consider putting him back in his habitat and opt for another. Nipping is okay, however. Unless of course tiny toothpick nips are too painful for you, but they shouldn't be as you're so large compared to a tiny hamster.

2) Pick a Ham, any Ham

We've discussed all the hamster options in Chapter One, but just in case you are still weighing your options, take a look at the following quick chart for Syrian hamster facts, facts about Teddy Bear hamsters, along with other hamster types.

"There is no reciprocity. Men love women, women love children, children love hamsters."

-Unknown

TYPE	COMMON NAME	ORIGIN	SIZE	LIFESTYLE	LIFE SPAN	COLORS
Syrian	- Golden - Teddy Bear - Standard - Fancy - Hamster Black Bear	Syria	10 – 17 cm (4-7 in)	Solitary after 10 weeks of age	2-2 ½ years	Wide Variety
Dwarf Campbell Russian	- Campbell - Djungarian - Russian	Asia	10 cm (4 in	Same sex pairs or groups	2 years	Wide Variety
Dwarf Winter White Russian	- Siberian - Djungarian	Russia, Asia	7-10 cm (3-4 in)	Same sex pairs or groups	2 years	Sapphire-pearl
Roborovski Dwarf	-Roborovski -Mongolian	Mongolia	2.5 – 5 cm (1-2 in)	Same sex pairs or groups	3 years	Wide Variety
Chinese	- Chinese striped hamster	China, Mongolia	10 cm (4 in)	Solitary	1-2 years	Brown backs, ivory coloring

Table 1: Characteristics of Hamster Breeds

3) MALE OR FEMALE? AND DETERMINING "HE" OR "SHE"

There are not a whole lot of discernable differences between male and female hamsters, other than the fact that females give birth.

Male hamsters don't (blessed is thy Hamster Lord, thank ye).

Is it Best to Buy Males and Females Together?

If you want hamster babies, then choose to buy a male and female hamster. Confirm with the owner that they are not siblings, however. If you do purchase a Syrian Hamster couple, even they will require separate living spaces when they are not breeding. Only during a short 12-hour window while the female is in heat will she permit the male to stay with her in her cage. You will need to keep them separate for the time they are not mating, which will add to your expenses.

If you prefer to have a cage of multiple hamsters, choose a communal brood such as one of the dwarf hamster varieties.

Which Gender is More Fun, Males or Females?

As far as activity levels go, both males and females are about the same. As far as aggressiveness and trainability, many hamster owners will tell you males are more tamable than females. Also, it is believed females have a greater propensity to bite.

This observation of females being the more aggressive gender may boil down to the fact that the female invests greater time and physical energy in rearing young. As such, she must focus more on protecting the nest and securing her offspring, thus making her more territorial.

Having said that, it is important to remember that all hamsters are individuals. You may end up with a bratty boy hamster, or a friendly female hamster. It all comes down to the individual and your relationship to him or her.

DETERMINING IF YOUR HAMSTER IS A "HE" OR A "SHE"

Unlike birds or other animal species, males and females are not distinguished by fancy plumage, bold colors, or muscle mass. However, male and female hamsters can tell who's who based on checking out each other's scent glands.

What, you don't understand how to identify male vs. female scent glands? Hmmm... okay. Well there is another way, although I've never examined hamsters myself via this method (considered extremely rude in the hamster world).

HOLD THE HAMSTER FIRMLY UPRIGHT BY THE SCRUFF:

Girls: The genital area and the anus, which basically look like two dashes are about ¼ inch apart. Female hamsters also have teats (7 or so pairs), but these may be difficult to spot on long-haired breeds such as Syrian hamsters.

Boys: The genital area and anus are farther apart, as much as ½ inch. In mature males, you will notice the penile area and testes may be visible, while the derrière is a bit fleshier.

AGE

As described earlier, hamsters have a short life span (as far as furless-giants are concerned). If you choose a more mature ham, keep in mind you have less time bonding with him.

So, what is the optimum age? Baby hamsters will not be sold younger than 5 weeks old. A hamster from 5 weeks old to 2 months old is a good age range to start. Hamsters older than two months are practically middle-aged.

These hams may be more difficult to bond with the owner and already entrenched in a living routine, thereby making them more anxious if uprooted.

How to tell the age?

Baby hams are small – about the size of your big toe. They have a rubbery texture and almost look like they were molded with wet clay.

Unlike furless-giants, hamster wheelchairs or canes have not been invented (yet) – so you can't spot the elderly by such devices. It's fairly easy checking signs for age. Look for patchy fur, frailty, and a lack of curiosity (which could also be a symptom of illness).

Hamster Styles

Sometimes shopping for a ham is like shopping for a hairstyle. Do you want hairless or longhaired? Curled or shorthaired?
What about color? Grey or yellow or violet? There are over 120 varieties of hairstyle and color). You basically have your pick from the hamster rainbow.

Personality

Of all the hamster types out there, Syrian hamsters are the easiest hamsters to socialize with humans. Winter Whites (which tend to nip) are also worth considering.

Just like furless-giants, all hamsters have their own personalities. Some hamster breeds are better known for nipping while others for friendliness. However, you cannot rule out a breed altogether because of the generalizations. Take each hamster on a case-by-case basis.

Syrian golden hamsters tend to be quite sociable with furless-giants and are also the hardiest of hamsters, able to withstand love even from children. However watch out when angered, we can get a bit nippy if upset.

Dwarf hamsters are known to be the most bitey of the hamsters.

Generally, they are not tame when taken out of the pet store.
This is simply a matter of taming your hamster once you bring him
home (see chapter 11 on taming). After he is comfortable with you
the nips may be less frequent or disappear altogether.
Winter Whites and Campbells are more in the middle; neither extremely sociable nor non-sociable.
Roborovskis are very timid, but can bond well if the owner is skilled
and patient.

As much as disposition depends on the individual hamster, the
personality match depends on the individual human as well! If your
hamster nips at you, don't panic.
Either pet him calmly or set him down back in the cage so he can
relax for a couple hours. Then try again!
The hamster will respond to your approach. If you are a calm per-
son, who doesn't over-react, than your hamster will likely follow
your lead. However, if you are anxious or nervous – than this will
only encourage our natural instinct´.

**INTERESTING FACT: A HAMSTER ISN'T NECESSARILY MEAN SPIR-
ITED IF HE NIPS AT YOU, AS THIS IS GENERALLY A SIGN OF NERV-
OUSNESS – NOT AGGRESSIVENESS. IN A PET SHOP, HAMSTERS ARE
MORE LIKELY TO NIP AT YOU WHEN HELD – DON'T TAKE IT TOO
PERSONALLY. INSTEAD, BE AWARE OF A HAMSTER THAT SEEMS
TIMID OR EXTREMELY SCARED. IN WHICH CASE, THE HAMSTER
MAY BE TOO DIFFICULT TO SOCIALIZE, AND QUITE POSSIBLY ILL.**

4) How to Select a Healthy Specimen

We will get much more into specific diseases later in the book, but
for now it's important to have a brief overview of what constitutes
good mental and physical health when choosing your pet hamster.
Here are some signs for health:

Teeth

Hamster teeth should show good alignment, the longer top incisors
should just overlap the lower teeth. This positioning ensures the
hamster's teeth will wear away naturally. Crooked or uneven teeth
may cause issues down the road, making it difficult for the hamster
to chew his food properly or stash morsels in his pouches.

Eyes

Furless-giants love hamsters for their bright, inquisitive eyes. Look
for a ham that has clean, bright eyes with no redness or discharge.
Of course, red eyes themselves are perfectly normal in some breeds
that have naturally pigmented red eyes.

Nose

A wet nose on a dog is a sign of health, but in a hamster a wet nose
is a big problem! Choose hamsters with dry noses.

Fur

A healthy coat has sleek and shiny with no bald patches.

Skin

Some signs of illness are not visible to the naked eye, which is why
it's so important to hold the hamster and examine him up close
before purchasing.

With your fingers, you will be able to run your hands lightly over his body. Anything but smooth and supple skin is a sign of disease. Scaly or rough skin suggests a fungal or parasite problem.

Older hamsters are also prone to cysts and tumors. While examining the skin, check for lumps and bumps.

Tail

Signs of dampness or diarrhea under the tail may be a disease called "wet tail" – fatal in 80 percent of hamsters who are afflicted with it.

Weight

You aren't looking for America's Next Top Model here. Hamsters are naturally plump. Bones protruding or a hamster wearing skinny jeans are signals the hamster is sick, old, or behind on fashion trends.

Posture

Healthy hamsters are sprightly and full of energy. If the hamster is curled up in a protective position while awake, she may be injured or ill. You want a hamster that will give you a great workout when you try to catch him if he escapes his cage (which he inevitably will).

Little Fella

[5]

Hamster Supplies

1) FROM CAGES TO CONDOS, HAMSTER REAL ESTATE

After food, this is my favorite chapter! Consider this the consumer reports of hamster gear.

With these insights, you will have insider knowledge to make the best first impression when you bring your new furry friend home. This information will help you with Golden Hamster care as well.

Hamster Real Estate

Just to reiterate because this is SO IMPORTANT: If you are getting a Syrian hamster (or Teddy Bear, or Black Bear hamster). Or if you are getting a Chinese dwarf hamster, these breeds must be kept alone!

If two adults of either breed are placed in a cage, they will fight until one of them dies. And you don't want that. Kapeesh? Kapeesh. As previously mentioned, Dwarf hamsters (the smaller hamsters) are communal. These include Campbell's Russian Dwarf hamster, Winter White or Siberian Dwarf hamsters, and Roborovski's Dwarf hamsters.

Because you will want to ensure the hamster's habitat is prepared and ready for your friend prior to their arrival, get your hamster properly outfitted with the following.

Cage Sizes

In the wild, a hamster burrow has many rooms and can be several feet underground. The domesticated hamster similarly prefers large spaces. If the cage is too small, your hamster may become bored, protective, and nippy.

Of the dozens of hamster cages sold at pet stores and online, many are not suitable for hamsters. A cage may be too small, unsafe, or impractical.

Always purchase the largest sized cage you can afford. Your hamster is a small, tiny thing compared to your 140 pound self; however don't scrimp on living space. The more room the better.

The numero uno tip for Syrian Hamsters care is to keep them separate. A golden Syrian hamster will feel caged in and cramped if housed in a cage smaller than 1858 cm2 (2 square feet).

Popular hamster cages for Syrian hamsters are those that allow you to build on later (i.e. tubes or platforms) as your wallet permits.

Primer on How Hamsters View the Cage

Some cages have rounded corners. The misconception is rounded corners are better for the hamster – that they will feel less caged in. However, few people understand hamsters cannot clearly perceive boundaries without a shadow cast. Rounded corners do not create a distinct shadow; thus making the hamster feel there is a dangerous drop off.

Imagine living over a 30 meter cliff (100 feet), and thinking you might step off it at any moment? You'd be pretty dizzy, huh? Choose a cage with straight corners so Mr. Hamster isn't under the impression he's walking on a tight rope.

Wire Cages

If you have a wire cage make sure the hamster cannot get through any of the holes between the wires. This is pretty obvious, but important to mention, as some of the dwarf varieties can be as small as 3-5 cm (1-2 inches).

Fish Tank

A glass fish tank with a wire mesh top is also a good option for a cage – as long as there are no more fish in it! (That's my little joke). There are drawbacks, however. With the glass walls the air doesn't circulate as well. Also, the contained size provides fewer options for add-ons and enrichment.

[5] | HAMSTER SUPPLIES

However, fish tanks are easier to clean and minimize odor (you still need to clean frequently to preserve the health of your hamster). They can be easier to escape from if you do not include lock clips on the screen. That's why the proper size for your tank should be a minimum 45 L (10-gallon).

BUILD YOUR OWN CAGE

With a little elbow grease, you can make a homemade hamster cage that is cheaper and much bigger than anything you can find in a pet store!

Things you'll need:

- large plastic bin
- electric drill with drill bits
- small hacksaw
- cloth
- ruler
- marker
- machine screws with nuts and washers (about 20 of each)
- Phillips screwdriver

Step 1. Select an appropriate sized bin for your hamster cage. 85 liters (90 quarts) works best.

Step 2. On the bottom side of the lid, mark the area you will cut out for the vent with a marker. Be sure to leave some space on each side for the cloth.

Step 3. Using the hand drill, drill two holes very close together so that they overlap. Do this at each corner. This will be the hole where the hacksaw will go through.

Step 4. Using a small hacksaw, cut along the lines you drew to cut out the piece of plastic from the lid.

Step 5. Take cloth and place it over the hole you just cut out of the lid to see how much cloth you will need.

Step 6. With scissors, cut out the amount of cloth required.

Step 7. Cut off any pieces that are sticking out of the cloth.

Step 8. Place the cloth over the hole and mark where you will need to drill for the machine screws. Do this along the entire edge every couple centimeters (or, every inch). Make sure to keep the hardware cloth in place to get accurate drilling spots.

Step 9. Drill out holes where you marked in step 8.

Step 10. Place a washer and machine screw on the bottom and secure it with a nut on the opposite side. Do this on four opposite sides to secure the cloth. Then screw in the remaining holes. Use a screwdriver if needed to fasten the bolts tight.

Step 11. Add accessories such as water, food bowl, and Syrian hamster toys.

2) Hamster Bedding

IMPORTANT: CEDAR OR CHLOROPHYLL SHAVINGS ARE BAD FOR HAMSTER'S LUNGS.

Most hamsters (especially Syrian) prefer recycled newspaper shreds. Disperse these throughout the cage and we'll collect the pieces we deem fit to create a nest with.

Carefresh is a popular brand, made from wood pulp fiber, it is a lightweight, fluffy bedding, although it is not very attractive in appearance. It is dust free and very absorbent, and has no inks or dyes and is biodegradable.

Although more difficult to clean, you can use recycled paper. Depending on what you shred (taxes, bills, junk mail) shredding the documents for your hamster to defecate on may be very satisfying.

3) Food Bowl and Water Bottle

Avoid plastic bowls as hamsters can easily chew them on. Opt for earthenware bowls.

Choose a water bottle with a ball bearing in the tube as these are less inclined to leak.

4) Hamster Enrichment

Hamsters require a variety of toys and accessories to stimulate their brains and prevent boredom. These items of course include hamster ball or wheel, but you can stimulate your brain as well through do-it-yourself accessories.

COCONUT HOME

Drain the liquid out of a coconut by making small holes in it. Set the coconut on a table and mark out the entrance for your hamster. Drill a 5 cm (2 inches) diameter hole where you want the entrance to be.

Remove the coconut flesh out (you may eat it as a snack and take a quick break)...

Okay, back to work. Now: clean and wash out the coconut. Sand down the edges to the door and voila! You have a fun little coconut nest your hamster will love to explore and sleep in.

HAMSTER TUBES

Toilet paper rolls can be used as fun tubs and tunnels for hamsters. I've never met a hamster that doesn't enjoy a new cardboard role! Bill, my old neighbor always used to show off when he got a new role. He would rub it in all our faces as if he got a new Porsche!

Hamsters love to explore paper roles, and even use them as mini-hideouts. Sometimes, their tasty chew toys as well. One might chew them up to smithereens and make a nest out of it. Inexpensive for you and fun for us!

HAMSTER MAZES

Once my furless-giant, Stevie, created a kind of palace for me. Shortly after the Holidays he had a lot of wrapping paper tubes lying around... there were even a few shoeboxes in the mix. He created a magnificent hamster maze taping together the tubes, shoe boxes, cereal boxes, and oatmeal containers. Oh my, I still have dreams what fun that was.

[6]

Make Room for your New Roommate

1) HAMS PREFER PRIVACY

So you're going to bring a rodent into your house. Congrats! Before
you do, hamster-proof your home. Consider these important
points. Location, location, location!

Hamsters prefer privacy in the wild. To feel secure with their living space, they need a dedicated hamster spot. Before bringing hammy home, think carefully about one location where the hamster's living space will remain within the house.

2) IDEAL TEMPERATURE

Housing should be placed in a room of constant temperature. Remember "Goldilocks and the Three Bears"? Neither too hot nor too cold, the temperature should be in the middle where it's just right.

Also, keep your hamster home away from direct sunlight and drafts. Us hamsters don't care much for tans or sunburns!

3) IS YOUR HOME HAMSTER-PROOF?

Okay, who let the dogs out? Is the hamster to be the only non-primate in the household? Dogs, cats, birds, snakes – keep your pets out of sight when hammy comes home for the first time.
At some point, you will want to set your hamster out of the cage so he can run free. Plan ahead and choose the room or enclosed space, but be sure there aren't any exposed wires or sharp-pointy things that can hurt little guys like us. Move all furniture in the house a good 10 cm (5 inches) away from the walls – just in case we do escape in an area we weren't supposed to. Hamsters will naturally want to go towards the wall or floorboard, where we feel more secure.

With the furniture moved away from the wall, your ham won't be pinned by the ugly ottoman in the corner no one sits in anymore. If your hamster does escape, you will want to be able to quickly secure your other pets so little hammy doesn't get eaten by the pink poodle named Florence. I would hate to have that in my obituary. How embarrassing!

The only task left is to come up with some cute and fun Black Bear names, Teddy Bear names, and Syrian Hamster names.

4) SYRIAN HAMSTER NAMES

You've heard about the four food groups, right? Well, when coming up with names for your Syrian hamster you have your choice from four "name-groups."

These include:

THE ADORABLE NAMES:

Hamster's are cute. We know it. You know it. So why not have a name that is as cute (okay... let's not kid ourselves... almost as cute) as your hamster?

Adorable names for Syrian hamsters include: Muffin, Snowy, Daisy, Cookie, Nibbles, Ping-Pong, Chew-Chew, or a name I don't recommend for your male hamster: Tu-Tu. For Teddy Bear hamster names, consider the ever popular: Fluffy, Hairy, or Fur-ball. Adorable Black Bear names to consider include: Blackie, Chocolate, and Hot Cocoa.

THE COMMON NAMES:

Not "adorable" but still pretty darn cute. Common Names include your average human names, such as: Bill, Steve, John, Lisa, Francis, or Dolly. Giving your Syrian Hamster a name like "Bob" certainly opens things up for comedic opportunities. Tell your friends you have to run home and "feed Bob." They'll probably assume you're talking about a grown Man who works at an office, and never in a million years guess that "Bob" is a hamster. Ha!

THE HUMOROUS NAMES:

Hamsters have great senses of humor, even if we are the butt of a joke. Choose a play on words, such as: Hammy, Ham-on-Rye, M.C Hamster... the options are endless!

THE IRONIC NAMES:

Give your furry friend a name like "Tiger" or "Spike" – sure, we don't look the part. But, the irony is awfully fun!

[7]

What's on the Menu?

1) Hamster Nutrition

Just like furless-giants, hamsters require a daily diet of food and water, although we tend to put healthier stuff in our bodies. I've seen the kinds of junk food Stevie eats when he gets home from school.

Cookies and Slurpees mostly – hamsters are smart enough to appreciate healthier fare. Does that make us more intelligent than the human species? You be the judge.

Through observation in the lab (unfortunately it had to be the lab, why not a hamster amusement park or happier place than a research facility?) humankind has developed an interesting and varied menu of commercially available products that appeal to Hamsters' nutritional needs and palate.

In the wild, us hamsters foraged for our food, storing seeds, nuts, and brush in our pouches to store for safekeeping. Now that we enjoy domestic life, our commercially prepared food reflects this aesthetic. And a bonus for us hamsters; commercial feeds are fortified with essential vitamins and minerals, making them possibly more nutritious than what we could find in the wild.

Hamster owners will find two types of food: seed mixes and extruded pellets.

Imagine if you had to eat the same thing everyday? It would drive you crazy, huh? Hamsters are the same in that they like some variety in life. A mixture of seed mixes and food pellets, garnished with the occasional treat is the best recipe for a happy hamster.

Nutritional Needs of Hamsters
Protein - 15 - 22%
Fat - 4 - 5%
Fiber - 10 - 15%

Feed Pellets

Hamster feed is available at your local pet store or online in 1-2 kilogram bags (~2-4 pounds). At the pet store, you may be persuaded to buy larger quantities at discount prices, but I advise you stay clear.

These cheaper feeds are often on the shelf longer, and their nutritional value suffers for it. Plus it tastes kind of nasty to us hamsters.

Not worth a hamster's cheek pouch, let me tell you. Hamsters like to graze and rarely eat a single meal in one sitting. Unlike furless-giants, our stomachs and brains work together in harmony. While your brain doesn't realize the stomach is full for 20 minutes, our brains are aware instantaneously.

How Much to Feed Your Hamster?

Feed your hamster one tablespoon of feed pellets per day, complimented with seeds and treats. Because we don't overeat, you can keep the food dish partially filled once a day.

Price for 1 kilogram (~2 pounds) of feed pellets?

Expect to spend approximately 4-6 L per kilogram (~$6-9 dollars per pound) of feed pellets. As a general rule, one kilogram (or 2 pounds) will supply your hamster enough food to last one month.

Food pellets are available from these brands (supplement with seeds and treats, further below):
- Oxbow
- Mazuri

INTERESTING FACT: FEED MIXES SHOULD CONTAIN 12-15 PERCENT PROTEIN AND 4-6 PERCENT FAT. IF YOU HAVE A FEMALE HAMSTER THAT IS NURSING HER BABIES, HOWEVER, SHE WILL REQUIRE MORE PROTEIN.

SEED MIXES

Seed mix is where things get really interesting for us hamsters. With so much variety colors and seed types, seed mixes are the trail mix of hamster fare. Seed mixes can be purchased as blends, or hamster owners can prepare their own.

Here's a list of some of the items found in your typical seed mix:
- Sunflower, apple, pumpkin seeds
- Corn
- Dehydrated carrots
- Split peas
- Pinto beans
- Millet, oats, wheat
- Raisins
- Folic acid
- Vitamins A and E

I'm drooling as I type this. The colors and flavors are endless. Plus, it's fun for us hamsters to forage through the mix, stashing the items we love in various parts of our cage for later. Just like our ancestors did in the wild!
However, there is a dark side to all the great diversity of seed mixes. Some items being tastier than others, your hamster may choose to eat only certain elements of the mix and ignore others; thereby missing out on some nutritional benefit the seed mix offered as a whole.

Food pellets, on the other hand are mashed up seed mixes in a solid form. Almost like a food pill or something an astronaut would eat in space. And if space food is anything like the rumor that precedes it, than it's boring. Until they get some nice restaurants in space, hamsters (and astronauts will prefer the seed mix to food pellets.

However, given the more balanced nutritional blend your hamster is likely to consume via food pellets, it's wise to make food pellets a large portion of your hamster's diet; with seed mixes as a supplement.

HOW MANY SEEDS TO GIVE YOUR HAMSTER?

- Sunflower seeds: Healthy, but should be fed in limited quantities (3 - 5 per day)
- Corn/Peas – Sugary. Strictly limit (1 - 2 kernels per week for Syrians and Robos, none for any other hamster species)
- Pumpkin seeds/peanuts - Fatty treats, limit (1 - 2 per week)

Seed mixes are available from these brands:
- Hazel Hamster
- Carefresh Complete

VITAMIN SUPPLEMENTS

Vitamin Supplements (such as A and E) can be added to seed mixtures, or even to water. This ensures your hamster is getting the nutrition he needs – in case he's a picky eater.
Furless-giants have the water cooler. Hamsters have the salt block, or salt lick. This is also a mineral supplement to our diet and can be hung from the side of our cage.

Sometimes salt licks are fortified with other minerals such as copper, iodine, and zinc. As long as there's salt in the lick, I'm satisfied. Now, there's even more in the way of mineral supplements. After this chapter you're going to get the impression hamsters are real health nuts! The final mineral supplement that cannot be overlooked is calcium. All living creatures need calcium to stay healthy. I know furless-giants take it all the time – and if you've never tried cricket–flavored calcium tabs. I highly recommend it.

2) Hamster H2O

Water. Ahhhhhhhh. It helps moves things along, break up food during digestion, and prevents dehydration. We like clean, fresh water so refill our water bottle constantly. If you don't have Perrier or Evian on hand, filtered tap water will do.

Keep your eyes peeled for slimy water bottles. Often the bottle spout is too narrow to hand wash, in which case the insides of the bottle get greenish and slimy. I really hate that, as all hamsters do. When this happens invest in a new bottle of water. We'd do the same for you!

How Often?

Change the hamster's food every day and their water every couple of days or sooner. The last thing you want to do is give green water to your hamster. This can and will cause illness.

3) Treats? (Yes, Please!)

Now, on to my favorite part: T-R-E-A-T-S.

You can give your hamster treats everyday. They're the element to the food recipe that adds that bit of gourmet.

Such tempting offerings include seed bars, often including a solid form of: dried fruit, flowers, vegetables, rose hips, carrots, and sweet potatoes.

There are crunchy treats – kind of like your potato chip – which include: sesame-coated peanut butter balls, yogurt chips, alfalfa, and hamster versions of fruit loops, life savers, and even ice cream! To top it all off, there is also something called the wooden chew stick, which looks like a giant toothpick. We like to gnaw on this thing and it comes in a delightful array of colors, shapes, and sizes.

Spoiler Alert!

Commercially produced treats often contain corn syrup as a bonding agent. This contains high amounts of sugar, and is no better for your hamster than it is for you.

HERE'S A LIST OF MY TOP FAV TREATS:

Apples

Bananas

Bread

Broccoli

Carrots

Cauliflower

Celery

Corn

Cottage cheese

Hard-boiled eggs

Grapes

Lettuce

Peanuts

Raisins

Boiled rice

Strawberries

Tomatoes

Yogurt

Crickets

Mealworms

The last two you may not have on hand, unless you're also an insect gourmand like us hamsters.

When filling your hamster's food bowl, make sure any treats are cut into 5 cm chunks (1 inch). Hamsters are not babies and do not require minced or purred food. We like to chew and gnaw at our food – it tastes better that way!

INTERESTING FACT: HAMSTERS AREN'T COWS, BUT WE CAN SURE EAT LIKE ONE! LEAVE A SMALL SUPPLY OF HAY (SUCH AS TIMOTHY AND ALFALFA) IN OUR CAGE EACH DAY. THIS GIVES US FIBER TO KEEP OUR DIGESTIVE PROCESSES RUNNING SMOOTHLY.

NOT ON THE MENU

Hamsters should abstain from the following:

- Unripe fruits or vegetables difficult for us to process.
- Canned fruits or vegetables (too much sugar and preservatives).
- Too many leafy greens, such as kale, spinach, romaine which gives us hamster cramps and diarrhea. Believe me, you do not want to get stuck cleaning the cage after your hamster eats dark greens...
We evolved in the wild to ration our food and look ahead. Often storing food up to several months. Keep this in mind when giving your hamster raw, fresh, and unprocessed cooked foods – we may hoard the items for a rainy day, beyond the advised "eat by" date. As such, perishables you treat your hamster should be given in moderation (and only once each day) so that any tasty treat your hamster hoards is less likely to spoil. By the way, are you gonna eat that?

INTERESTING FACT: A HAMSTER CAN STUFF HIS CHEEKS FULLER THAN THE SIZE OF HIS OWN HEAD, AND WITH A QUANTITY OF FOOD THAT EQUALS HIS OWN BODY WEIGHT! I'VE SEEN SOME FURLESS GIANTS THAT HAVE COME PRETTY CLOSE TO THIS REMARKABLE FEAT AS WELL!

4) DEAR, DIARY: BOTTOMLESS CHEEK POUCHES

Hamsters are blessed with exquisite cheeks – the most remarkable thing about our hamster jowls is that just when you think you are out of room, you can make your cheeks expand like a balloon!

Our cheeks are basically like gigantic pockets that extend from our shoulders to the top of our head. When I was young, my siblings and I would often enjoy contests to see who could stuff the most in their cheeks.

My sister Omelet and my brother Jambon would go head-to-head, or "cheek-to-check" – stuffing our faces literally to the brim. One day, I was able to stuff 107 food pellets into my cheek pouches. Omelet stuffed 78, and Jambon stuffed 63. Jambon actually got off to a great start... stuffing more pellets than Omelet and myself; however he was hungry. He couldn't stop eating! I was proclaimed the winner.

What does the winner receive? Food pellets. 248 to be exact. Sure, some of them were slightly wet with salvia being in my siblings' mouths... but no matter. I stashed them away in my nest – a special corner of our communal cage. At night, I'd rest my head above the pellets and have sweet dreams of victory.

Have you seen that show "Hoarders?" I don't watch much t.v, I catch glimpses when Stevie tunes into the show occasionally. Anyway, humans are hoarders on so many levels. Newspapers. Clothing. Shoes. Stamps. Even vintage oil cans! (Apparently that's worth something)?

What I can't understand is how humans can hoard all that stuff in their puny cheek pouches. Maybe one day a human creature will explain it to me?

I keep meaning to ask my human, Stevie, how many food pellets can he stuff into his cheek pouches? I'm not sure how he would reply, but surely he cannot stuff as much as me.

[8]

Hamster Hobbies

1) FITNESS JUNKIES

Aside from nutritional needs, hamsters require vigorous exercise in daily life to stay fit and happy. A stimulating jog on our wheel can make the blues go away, and also enriches our daily lives.

Plus, us hamsters look great in a hamster Speedo.

Yoink! Just kidding...

INTERESTING FACT: IN THE WILD, HAMSTERS CAN RUN UP TO 8 MILES IN A DAY IN SEARCH OF FOOD OR A NEW HOME. HOW MANY MILES CAN YOU DO?

2) SETTING UP THE HOME GYM

EXERCISE WHEELS

The Soloflex of hamster equipment, exercise wheels come in a variety of styles and sizes. From the petite 14 cm wheel to the monster 36 cm (5 ½ inches to 14 inches). From slatted to solid plastic. From the grip basic to the "comfort wheel" – a top of the line wheel made from solid plastic, which doesn't have a grip, so your hamster need not turn the wheel with his claws. And when tired, he may rest at the base of the wheel for a breather.

HAMSTER BALL

And finally, a closed wheel suspended in a chariot so the hamster can navigate around a room. This a nice exercise option when your ham wants to get out of his cage and go for a mobile run. Be advised, your hamster can enjoy this method for twenty minutes max. Anything beyond is too grueling considering the limited ventilations and no access to water.

3) HOBBIES AND OTHER DISTRACTIONS

Of course hamsters enjoy many hobbies, from mazes to burrowing. One often-overlooked hobby is hamster racing.

Hamster Racing

In the United Kingdom during 2001, an epidemic of foot and mouth disease squashed the horse-betting season. Lovers of the sport opted to institute an alternative and came up with hamster racing.

The sport has since made a splash in the U.S. and Asia. All hamsters can get involved, with two divisions available: Syrians and Dwarfs. All is needed is a locomotive of some kind (usually a hamster ball) and a hamster with particularly large forelegs.

4) Quick Note on Children

If you have children, be on the lookout during children and hamster playtime. Children can be great cuddlers – but not when they squeeze the living life out of you or accidently poke your eyeballs out. So keep your kiddies on a leash, ok? The dog is on one and I trust him a heck of a lot more.

Little Fella

[9]

Hamster on the Loose!

1) HAMSTER HOUDINIS

No point ignoring the inevitable: all hamsters will at some point escape their cage or your grip (if you are in the middle of a petting session) and run amuck! Don't take it personally. Your hamster isn't trying to run away and work professionally as a hamster Houdini. He may have simply gone foraging! After all, it's our instinct.

Given time and patience, your hammy will most likely mosey on back to his burrow regardless of what your next move is. However, there are a lot of dangers in the furless-giant's household. It's built to accommodate your needs, but not your hamsters.

Anyone with young children knows the importance of "child-proofing" their home. Like children, us hamsters are a curious bunch. We're bound to explore the areas you had hoped we wouldn't notice. Here are some steps to take to hamster-proof your home in case your hamster gets on the loose:

- Homeowners who've been so lucky to have visitors of the mice our rat persuasion are familiar with a rodent's love affair with wires. Your hamster is no different. Ensure all electrical cords are out of reach, otherwise your hamster may be tempted to chew on what looks like delicious taffy.

- Seal off cracks in floors, walls, and any openings in appliances. Gaps that may look non-existent to you are wide open spaces to your tiny hamster. When in doubt how to fill a crack, seal off with electrical tape.- Wood and paper are tasty morsels to your hamster. Move these items out of reach, or consider spraying with an animal repellant such as Pet Off or Bitter Apple.

- Your hamster loves greens. Houseplants resemble salad bowls – so why tempt us with plants within easy-to-reach places? Unless you are absolutely sure your plants are not poisonous, it's a good idea to place them in at higher elevations.

- Keep household cleaners and chemicals hidden. One whiff of the stuff in your hamster's delicate lungs and he'll turn blue – forever. And that's a morph he would rather not have.

- Keep all drawers, lids, closets, buckets, and boxes closed.

- Cover toaster slats.

- Pull furniture away from the wall so that your hamster doesn't himself stuck behind the enormous hutch.

- Check that baseboards are secured on the wall.

- Confirm sharp objects do not protrude out of the walls.

NOTICES FOR YOU TO KEEP THE CHECKLIST IN MIND:

_____

_____

_____

_____

_____

_____

_____

_____

This laundry list of items may be overwhelming – but it will save you the headache of scrambling to secure your home when your hamster is loose. Remember: as a hamster guardian, it's your responsibility to ensure your home's safety for the little guy. He is not familiar with the ways of big city life in your kitchen and living room.

Not if, when... your hamster escapes, ensure all of the above is taken care of. Also, if you happen to be in the middle of cooking, say scrambling eggs perhaps; turn off the stove and all burners, unless you want your next meal to be a hamster omelet.

2) How to Bring him Back?

What do all animals have in common? We love treats.
Hopefully by this time, you've spent enough one-on-one with your hamster to have an idea of his favorite munchies. These treats can be used as bait to lure your ham out of his hiding spot during his sojourn in your home.

Much like a zombie invasion, here is your step-by-step course of action to take when your ham is missing.

1. Clear the room of any other pets so there is no chance your hamster will be captured, maimed, injured, or killed by a helpful dog, cat, bird, snake or otherwise.

2. Do you have any nervous adults or children nearby? Quarantine them in another room. The fewer bodies the better: more room for you to maneuver, and less anxiety for your pet hamster.

3. Find a good box or bucket (ensure it's empty, of course) and leave it in a corner of the room or somewhere your hamster can easily get to.

4. Now for the bait: set-up a trail of your hamster's favorite treats leading up to the box. No doubt this will wet his appetite. As he forages for the treat he will end up right where you want him.

INTERESTING FACT: HAMSTERS (AND LIONS AND SHARKS AND JUST ABOUT ANY OTHER ANIMAL EXCEPT HUMANS) SMELL FEAR. HAMSTERS ARE FAMILIAR WITH YOUR SCENT. ANY FEELINGS OF ANXIETY OR ANXIOUSNESS WILL BE COMMUNICATED TO YOUR HAMSTER THROUGH YOUR SCENT. THIS IS WHY ITS SO IMPORTANT TO ASK SCARED LOVED ONES TO DISAPPEAR, AND FOR YOU ABOVE ALL, TO STAY CALM.

[10]

Nitty Gritty: Syrian Hamster Care

1) HAMSTER BATHROOM

It's not all roses rooming with a hamster. Sure, us furry fellows are cute and cuddly.

The way we crinkle our noses and run on the tread-wheel. At this point you're thinking, "what's not to love?" Well, we have needs too. Just like all animals. Toiletry needs...

Although Syrian hamsters are not naturally smelly, Syrian hamster cages can be if housecleaning doesn't keep up on it for us <wink> <wink>.

During your hamster's tenure, you will wear many hats: Parent, buddy, maid, and plumber... So let's get to it, shall we?

2) CLEANING-OUT SYRIAN HAMSTER CAGES

Did you know many hamster illnesses are caused by containments found in dirty cages? By cleaning your hamster's living space regularly, you are helping your hamster live a long and healthy life.

EVERYDAY...

On a daily basis, you will want to remove any soiled litter and wet bedding from the cage. This will minimize offensive urine smells from your hamster's home, and yours as well!

Remember that fruit or vegetable you offered as a treat yesterday? Your hamster probably stashed it in a corner for safe-keeping. You will want to remove this each day as well. This requires just a moment of your time each day, so do it!

EVERY WEEK...

At least once per week, you will need to clean your hamster's cage. The first couple times you clean the cage, you may feel awkward. And probably spend way more time than you bargained for! But with practice, you will be a cage-cleaning pro!

Before you begin the process, make sure you have temporary housing in place. Your little friend will need a safe and secure spot to loiter while you get down to business.

Consider letting your hamster run in his hamster ball while you clean. Many hamster owners will plug the bathtub and let their hamster storm the tub in his ball. It provides entertainment for both hamster and human. While hammy is on a little vacay, you are gettin' it done.

As mentioned previously, hamsters must not remain in the ball longer than twenty minutes. If you think it may take longer, or if you prefer to put your hamster elsewhere; a shallow box, or even an empty bucket or wastebasket will do (of course, this doesn't sound nearly as exciting to us our hamster ball).

Hamster-Home Layout, 101

To you your hamster's home is a disorganized mess. To us hamsters, we have clear partitions. We have our toilet quarters; call it the "lavatory." In another corner, we prefer to stash our food, call it our "pantry." And finally, another corner we enjoy grooming, call it our "boudoir."

Hamsters naturally pee in one place, so we help on cleaning. (I must apologize however, on behalf of all hamsters as we do not poop in one place. Sorry).

The Toilet

Wear disposable gloves so your hands remain clean. All set? Good! For starters, you will want to clean the toilet or "bedding." If you are using a hamster toilet (often a plastic mayonnaise jar will do) remove the jar and soak it in hot water and mild soap. You can also put vinegar in the water. It removes the smell and when it is washed off and it leaves no scent.

However, sometimes no matter how good you are about cleaning, the urine smell can stick anyway. If the urine smell isn't removed, pour in some baking soda into the water as well.

If you aren't using a jar for the toilet and simply have the nest in the cage, remove the bedding in the hamster cage. Unclip the base of the cage and replace it with a plastic bag – this will make cleanup a breeze. Then, shuffle most of the bedding into the bag – but don't remove all of it. Set aside a small portion of the bedding to use later. Explanation forthcoming.

THE PANTRY

As burrowers, your hamster has likely hidden secret stashes of food in various parts of his home. Don't leave any food scraps behind in the cage. Don't worry, your hamster won't mind so much and can build again. The last thing you want is a rotten egg from last Easter stowed away in a crevice somewhere... hamster and human alike don't like to smell the likes of that.

LIVING ROOM

Next, remove all the toys, tunnels, wheels, food bowl, and various plastic accessories from the cage and set aside. Note* never clean wood, cloth or porous materials with water as they will stay damp and grow moldy.

Do you have any wooden chew toys? If so, keep tabs on how long they've been in your hamster's cage. It's advised all wooden playthings are thrown out after one month's use.

Using mild soap and warm water clean the items and dry them. Next, clean the cage from top to bottom. Be sure that any perfumes or odors from the soap are gone completely. Hamsters are very sensitive to scents and prefer an odorless cage – so don't think you're doing your hamster favors by using the fancy shmancy "basil-lavender-breeze" scented soap. Unless of course, your hamster is French.

So, is everything clean and more importantly, dry? (Wet items encourage mold and may cause illness, so dry everything really well!) If so, now it's time for the fun part: you get to play decorator!

INTERESTING FACT: A HAMSTER'S SENSE OF SMELL IS HIGHLY ACUTE. WE'RE PRACTICALLY BLIND AND NEED TO FIND OUR WAY AROUND SOMEHOW! BY DEPOSITING OUR PERSONAL EAU DE HAMSTER VIA OUR SEBACEOUS GLANDS, WE ARE ABLE TO LOCATE VARIOUS POINTS OF INTEREST IN THE WILD AND IN OUR DOMESTIC HOMES AS WELL. THAT'S WHY IT'S SO IMPORTANT TO FORGO THE HARSH BLEACH AND CHEMICALLY LADEN CLEANING PRODUCTS. THESE SCENTS WIPE THE SLATE CLEAN AND CONFUSE THE HECK OUT OF US BLIND-AS-BAT HAMS.

The Same, But Different

Add fresh bedding to the cage. Scatter it throughout (your ham will gather it himself and make a new nest). Remember that small portion of old bedding you set aside? It's time to add that back to the cage too where the old nest was. Your hamster will appreciate something familiar from his old home. The scent of the old bedding will make him feel more comfortable and will let him know that the space is still truly his territory.

You may think your hamster prefers the toys and accessories to be left exactly as they found it. Wrong! We're the most curious of fellows and appreciate a little spice in our lives. Shake our home up a bit and place our toys in different spots in the cage. When your ham returns, he'll enjoy playing Sherlock Holmes and rediscover where his items are located. You know, it's like when you lose your keys, and spend hours looking for them? Only fun.

So, How do you Like the Place?

When you reunite your hamster to his home, leave him alone for several hours. This is not a time to play. He needs to acclimate to his environment and make the space his own.

It's kind of like when you move to a new house or apartment, you want to get your items set up and organize. Packing boxes and clutter make you nervous, so respect!

Sometimes there are Exceptions: Cleaning the Cage

As with all things, there are exceptions to the rule. Your hamster is as unique as you are, and they may prefer cleaning routines with greater or less frequency.

Because hamsters rely on their sense of smell to navigate around the cage, they may be stressed out each week after the cage is clean. How do you know if your hamster is finding it difficult to adjust to a clean cage? You will be able to tell by how quickly it gets dirty once again. The hamster will work extra hard to deposit his scent everywhere, and that means going to the bathroom as frequently as possible to get his smell back into the cage.

3) Tips to Reduce Odors

Pee-Uuuuu! Inevitably you're going to get some smells emanate from the cage now and then.

Products

Stevie has Carefresh Ultra in my personal residence. This bedding material is cotton-white, so any areas your hamster peed are easily spot-able. This helps cut down your time removing the soiled bedding litter considerably.

Ensure you are using highly absorbent materials. Other bedding materials include: torn up paper, shredded cardboard, and commercial paper pellets.

POTTY TRAIN

An easy way to reduce urine odor is train your hamster to use the bathroom. Not your bathroom, silly – a homemade hamster toilet! Read more at the end of this section.

NEW CAGE

Consider upsizing. Invest your bucks in an extra-roomy cage for your hamster. The little hamster cages sold in pet stores get odorous fast. The bigger the cage, the less concentrated the urine smell will be.

To curb costs, try to score a ferret, chinchilla, or rat cage, which are often available inexpensively second-hand. *Be sure to clean it thoroughly first so as the other animal's scent doesn't stress out your hamster.

POTTY TRAIN

Train your friend to use the toilet. Hamsters prefer to urinate in the same spot, so you can simply make this instinct easier to grasp by using a litter tray or plastic/glass jar.

First, find a small and sturdy plastic container with a lid such as an empty pickle or mayonnaise jar. Make sure the jar is large enough so your hamster has room to turn around in.

Then, cut a 5 to 7.5 cm (2 to 3 inches) diameter hole in the side of the container. For dwarf hamsters, cut a hole about 2.5 cm (1 inch) – this will ensure that litter won't scatter when the hamster is finished doing his dirty work.

Finally, sand the edge of the hole you made smooth for safe entries and exits.

You may choose to replace this homemade hamster potty every few months, or after the plastic absorbs the urine odor (or after your hamster shows interest in gnawing the material, whichever comes first).

If your hamster likes to chew on things, then opt for a glass potty – in which case, use a 500 ml (1-pint) wide mouth jar. For a dwarf hamster, use a 250 ml (1/2 pint) jam jar.

So How does this Work? (Hamster diapers not required)

Cover the bottom of the potty with litter and add some urine-soaked bedding along with a few droppings. Your hamster will recognize the smell as his, and when it's time to relieve himself; his natural instinct will be to go where he's gone before.

Put the hamster potty in a corner of the cage your hamster has approved already as the toilet. When your ham is awake, place him at the outhouse opening so that he can get a whiff of what's inside.

Never force your hamster into the potty. Most hamsters eventually catch on; after all it's not rocket science, duh! Once your hamster is regularly using the plastic "potty," simply empty it each day and add fresh substrate.

If the Cage is still Odorous

If the hamster cage still smells bad despite a good cleaning, it may not be the cage that emits the offensive odor, but possibly your hamster.

Illnesses such as wet tail (and others described in chapter twelve) can smell like the worse body odor you've ever whiffed. Make an appointment with your vet immediately so as to ensure your hamster is properly treated.

A FINAL NOTE ON BEDDING PRODUCTS

Do not use: bathing dust, kitty litter, or cedar shavings (which cause allergic reactions). The small particles will irritate your hamster's lungs. And the kitty litter pieces may injure his little feet.

Also, remember we're a curious bunch – whatever you put in our home, we'll try nibbling a bit to see if it's tasty. This goes for plastic toys, wood chips, and kitty litter (which is toxic to hamsters).

Straw should also be avoided as the sharp ends may cause injury to the hamster's eyes or cheek pouches.

The best bedding for hamsters is paper based bedding like toilet paper or tissue paper. Syrian Hamsters and Dwarf Hamsters love paper bedding!

QUICK NOTE ON CLEANING TIMES:

ITEM	FREQUENCY
Food Bowl	Every other day
Water Bottle	Every other day
Toys	Once per week
Bedding	Remove soiled bedding every day and replace the nest once per week (twice per week if smelly).
Cage	Once per week

Table 2: Hamster Cleaning Frequency

[11]

Inside the Hamster Mind

1. Discern Body Behavior

Furless-giants seem to have a pretty good handle on deciphering body language among their own species. Of course the nuances of smiles, winks, frowns... it's all Greek to me! But show me a hamster with a crinkle in his nose or a twitch of his ear, and I can tell you exactly what that hamster has on his mind.

What are the body language hot spots on a hamster? The nose, ears, whiskers, and eyes.

You'll notice, when two or more hamsters meet for the first time, they will sniff and circle one another to determine sex and dominance. After they have a handle on who's who, they'll decide if they want to relax, pick an argument, or fight!

HAMSTER POSTURES

Of course hamsters are unique and have their own personal ways of communicating. As with furless-giants, certain gestures are unanimous among hamster body language.

If your hamster is happy – you will most often witness typical grooming, stretching, or yawning behaviors. If he is feeling particularly exuberant (more typical with Dwarf Russian Hamsters), he may put on a show for you! Said show will include climbing on objects in his cage like a madman, and maybe even share a forward summersault or back flip for you! I think that earns a treat, don't you?

CURIOUS AND INTERESTED

There are many gestures your hamster will use to express curiosity and interest. One of the most common behaviors is the lick. Unlike dogs, which lick to display affection or submission; a hamster lick is not so personal. We're merely trying to determine if you are a tasty morsel we can chew on.

Hopefully, after one lick your hamster will be able to figure out that you are not food and won't need to take a nibble to make sure. However, we may take a couple more licks because we enjoy the salty taste. It's okay, go about your business. Never mind us...

BODY BEHAVIOR	WHAT IT MEANS
Erect on hind legs, nose in air, ears pricked	Smells good, is it time for my 5 o'clock carrot?
Erect ears, twitching nose and whiskers	Curious, eager to play

Table 3 Hamster behaviors Confident and Relaxed

If your hamster is comfortable in his home, most behaviors you'll notice are contented, calm behaviors such as grooming and stretching.

You'll see us lick our paws and comb our faces and fur. If we're social and living with other hamsters, we may groom one another.

BODY BEHAVIOR	WHAT IT MEANS
Periodic grooming and stretching	At ease
Loud clicking noises with teeth, known as Bruxing	Relaxed, also may occur while sleeping

Table 4 – Hamster behaviors

ANXIOUS

Hamsters will always pack their cheek pouches with some food and then go off to store it for later; it is what we are best known for. However, sometimes when we're particularly anxious, we may fill our pouches with enough food to feed an entire country full of hamsters. In which case, we may be feeling insecure or need extra love and attention.

BODY BEHAVIOR	WHAT IT MEANS
Constant grooming and stretching	Too much grooming is a sign something is wrong. Either we're not feeling welcome in our cage and need to deposit our scent obsessively, or may be sick

Table 5 – Hamster Behaviors Angry and/or Frightened

Sometimes behaviors that exhibit fear are the same ones that exhibit anger. You will have to use your best judgment to determine what we are emoting. Best advice? Leave us be when we show off our fangs or roll on our backs.

BODY BEHAVIOR	WHAT IT MEANS
Ears tilted forward, cheeks puffed out, teeth bared	Ready to fight, or just plain scared
Erect on hind legs, teeth bared	Aggressive, put up your dukes!
Biting	Scared or angry, give us some space

Table 6 – Hamster behaviors

Feelings of Dread

If you were in a small space and couldn't escape on your own free will, you may sometimes feel dread too. Best thing to do when we work ourselves up in these states is to leave us be.

BODY BEHAVIOR	WHAT IT MEANS
Ears back, posture stiff	Dread or defense
Cowering	Fearful
Running, interspersed with grooming	Agitated

Table 7 – Hamster behaviors

AMOROUS

Great for breeders, and downright uncomfortable for non-breeders – when in heat, your female hamster may sometimes exhibit romantic displays of affection. Your Syrian female may stand still, with her head forward and raise her tail while she enjoys a friendly stroke.

She's letting you know she is receptive for a bit of male Syrian company. Of course, if you aren't a breeder or do not want a litter of hamster kiddies in 12 weeks, than the poor Missus will remain unrequited. That's okay, after twelve hours she will no longer be in the mood.

TERRITORY

Both male and female Syrian hamsters have scent glands, which are located over the hips. Your Syrian hamster will often rub his hips or slide himself along the cage floor and other objects. Possibly this will happen after a cage cleaning or when your hamster has been moved to new housing and he feels the need to mark his area as his territory.

Sure, it seems silly – after all, we Syrians live alone; so why would we expect unwelcome company? But hey, I do it. My friends do it. It's in our DNA and goes way back to when we lived in the wild. Old habits die hard, you know?

BITING

On the positive side we hamsters rarely bite – to avoid a sharp nip, always hold us gently. In the case of Syrian Hamsters (we tend to respond with a more prolonged, will not let go type bite), handle us gently and avoid any sudden movements.

MISCELLANEOUS POSTURES

BODY BEHAVIOR	WHAT IT MEANS
Walking stiff legged, back arched	Sign of submission
Chewing on cage bars	Boredom, get new toys or a bigger cage
Eyes barely open, ears laid back	Sleepy, give him some space

Table 8 – Hamster Behaviors

HAMSTER VOCALIZATIONS – SQUEAKS, SNIFFLES, AND TEETH CLICKING

Most noises us hamsters make are not even discernable by your ears. You are missing out on a lot of cool sounds, let me tell you. So, for this section I'll just touch on the few sounds you actually can hear. Too bad, this is just the tip of the iceberg for the squeaks, squeals, and growls we're capable of.

You may sit in another room and overhear your hamster making various noises. Find comfort in knowing that none of these sounds are signs of aggression as the hamster is by himself. It's most likely just the usual squeaks and squeals they make while tinkering around in their cage.

Hamsters will sometimes squeak when they're scared or in pain. Or they may be vocal when they're exploring a freshly cleaned cage. Often these squeaks are simply explanations of joy – as in "wow, what's this I don't remember seeing it here before!"

Sometimes, when I am very relaxed, I'll utter simple signs of pleasure or winding down noises when I turn in for a nap.

Sniffing noises are probably the most frequent sounds you will hear a hamster make.

Remember, our eyesight is so poor, we rely on our sense of smell and will often be heard sniffing our cage, or even sniffing you to get an idea of our environment.

Chattering

If your hamster is chattering his teeth, it's a sign that he is excited or nervous, and in some cases this may be a sign of aggression or fear.

Loud Squeaks

The little guy may feel discomfort (check to make sure he's not injured), or agitated. Of course, he could just want attention.

Hissing

The hamster is upset or frightened.

Clicking

Happy and content.

Teeth Grinding

Your ham is irritated and wishes to be left alone. Better leave him be before you upset him further.

2) Problem Behavior

There are a variety of problem behaviors you may observe. Usually these behaviors signal an issue that you might be able to fix quite easily.

Problem: Excessive Wheel Use

The average hamster runs 8 miles a day. However, your cute dwarf hamster, Millie, may run 20 miles a day. This is excessive wheel use and may indicate poor Millie feels confined or bored.

SOLUTION: Purchase a larger cage to give Millie more space. If she already has a decent cage size, perhaps introducing more environmental enrichments and activities to her space may engage Millie more physically and decrease the abuse of the wheel. Hamsters would much prefer expelling their energy running around a more spacious cage or actively interacting with enrichments.

PROBLEM: FOOD MARKING

Hamsters are natural food hoarders. While you clean the cage, you of course remove the perishable food and bits from the freshly cleaned cage. However, for some hamsters this makes them very neurotic.

Your hamster may view their cage as unsafe, and consider perhaps a predator or scavengers are in their midst, removing their precious food supply they have painstakingly stored for future use, and they must thereby proclaim the food they store by urinating on it. This is a territorial behavior. Some even resort to storing food in their toilet corner in order to keep it safe from scavengers.

SOLUTION: Remove only moldy pieces of food from the cage and allow your hamster to hoard the dry food, or perishable foods that have not yet exceeded their expiration date. Perhaps in the future you can remove more of the food, but as long as it's not moldy or stinks then leave it to your hamster to hoard and his food marking will soon cease.

PROBLEM: NEST ABANDONMENT

To us hamsters, the nest is sacred. It is as important as food and water. We're driven by a "nesting instinct" and have a clear desire to protect it. If your hamster suddenly abandons their nest, it is a sign they are feeling anxious.

If your hamster has abandoned their usual sleeping quarters for seemingly no apparent reason, you have disturbed the nest too much during cleaning. In the hamster's eyes, their secret nesting spot has been "discovered" and they must nest in a more inaccessible place (such as a wheel or tunnel).

SOLUTION: Always include a bit of the old nest bedding when cleaning the cage or introducing a new nesting site. The hamster will recognize their scent and consider the nesting site safe from predators.

The new nesting material you introduce to the cage should be placed anywhere in the cage but the nest. Allow your hamster to "find" this new nesting material and take it back to his nest. This should alleviate any undue stress.

Problem: Eating Poop

Rodents eat their own poop because their diet of plants is hard to digest efficiently, and they have to make two passes at it to get everything out of the meal.

You've probably heard of cows chewing their cud? It's similar to that, only cows can re-eat their food without having to poop it out first.

Rodents eat their poop also because it contains vitamins produced by their intestinal bacteria. Vitamins we are unable to absorb through the intestinal wall, but we can get at them through eating our poop.

SOLUTION: Deal with it, or don't watch!

Problem: Aggressive Females

At times female hamsters may be overly aggressive of their territory.

This may occur when the female is in heat. The reason most likely is she is psychologically preparing her nest for her "babies" this may happen whether she is pregnant or not), and wants to ensure supreme safety of her territory as she has more of a parental investment.

SOLUTION: Nothing much you can do but let time pass. Hold off on cleaning the cage for every two weeks, and simply remove soiled bedding from the cage.

PROBLEM: FEMALES EATING THEIR YOUNG

Okay, this is something that probably sounds extremely cruel to other species, but to hamsters it is an unfortunate scenario that does come up.

Baby hamsters, or "pups" are very small and frail. While adult hamsters are blind as bats, pups are even more blind. As any good Mother does, Mother hamsters protect their offspring. And if there is a threat to the pup that could possibly kill or harm them, or if they feel they have been attacked, they will kill and eat the pups if they feel there is very little they can do to protect their young.

SOLUTION: If you find a few pups of the litter have been killed and/or eaten, there are steps you can take to prevent more deaths:

- Mothers need extra protein for lactation. Make sure there are high protein foods available immediately before and after birth.

- Avoid handling babies. Your scent on the pups may confuse the Mother – she either will think her pups are a food source, or consider them not her own due to your scent.

- Sometimes Mothers will eat their young when there is not enough food to support the litter size. Make sure her cage is as large as possible, with extra food during the pregnancy.

3) TAMING AND TRAINING

Yeah, we're adorable and you want to cuddle with us. Maybe not off the bat, but eventually after we gain your trust, we will want to cuddle with you too!

Here are some surefire steps to get you and your hamster acquainted so the cuddle-a-thon can begin.

HANDLING YOUR HAMSTER FOR THE FIRST TIME

If you bring your hamster home for the first time, hold off picking him up for a good week so he gets accustomed to his surroundings.

Don't try to handle your hamster during the day when they are most likely sleeping. Introduce handling your hamster after he has emerged from his nest on his own – most likely in the evening.

Step 1. After bringing your hamster home, hold off a week and wait to pick him up after he is eating, drinking, and playing in your presence.

Step 2. Spend time around your hamster outside his cage. Talk quietly with him and even sing to him. If you're at a loss for words, pick up a book and read aloud.

Step 3. Bribe your hamster with treats, such as sunflower seeds or dried fruits by hand. Begin by offering treats between the bars of his cage, once your hamster scurries in your direction for the treats, put your hand just inside the cage. However, don't try to touch your hamster, always give him space and allow him to make the first move. When he feels comfortable, he will approach your hand and give it a good sniff. This may take a few tries.

Step 4. If you have a bathtub, you can sit in a dry bathtub (make sure the drain is plugged) with the cage. Open the door of the cage and let the hamster come out to explore the terrain. You can use treats to make things more interesting for him.
You can use this opportunity to clean the cage while he scurries around in the tub, or simply sit in the tub with him so he gets used to your presence.

Step 5. By now you probably have a good idea what kinds of treats your hamster enjoys. Place a treat in your open hand at one end of the cage. With time, your hamster will eventually come to your hand – place his paws on your palm and reach for the treat.

Step 6. Once your hamster is actively crawling up you're your hand for the treat, scoop him up and bring him out of the cage.

The first couple of times, the hamster will jump off – eventually however, he will realize there is no harm hanging out on the hand-elevator and will feel safe.

The timing for each step varies from hamster to human. The important thing to remember is to be patient and always calm. Never push yourself onto the hamster, allow him to come to you. Only he knows when he's comfortable and trusts you.

How to Pick up a Hamster

The best way to pick up your hamster is scooping him up with one hand, and cupping the palm of your hand with the other to prevent him from jumping off. After all, it's a long way down – and with our poor eyesight, we really can't determine how high we're up!

Eventually your hamster can crawl from hand to hand and arm to arm. You can keep him occupied and stress-free through the bribery method (works for me!)

How to Pick up a Hamster that isn't Tame

When shopping for your hamster, or early on when you are first getting to know your hamster, you will likely have to pick up a hamster that isn't used to your scent. An easy way to keep the stress levels low is to place a cup on its side in front of the hamster and gently herd him into the cup. Because we're so curious, we will likely walk right in without an invitation!

When Holding your Hamster

Your hamster may make sniffing sounds while you hold him. He may even flinch away because he is startled. Hamsters have poor eyesight, and when you reach your hand in for a stroke, we don't see your hand coming until it's directly in front of our face.

Instead of stroking immediately pick him up and stroke him. Simply put your hand in the bedding and allow your hamster to come to you. This way, you will not surprise him with a hand just suddenly in his face. Also, when you pick him up, don't do so from the top - scoop him up. No one likes a scary, disembodied hand coming down from overhead.

[12]

Recognizing a Sick Hamster

1) RECOGNIZE A SICK HAMSTER

This chapter gets me neurotic. There are about a thousand things that can go wrong with the hamster body, and when I start researching one, I assume I have it. So here goes!

Sick hamsters will groom excessively, refuse to eat, refuse to leave the nest, or make noises that tell you something is wrong. Hopefully by now you've established a rapport with your hamster and can recognize when he needs help.

Here's a rundown of the many things that can fail in the hamster body, from your run of the mill colds to strokes.

2) Hamster Illnesses

Colds

Sneezing, wet nose, heavy breathing, or sitting in a hunched position is a sign your hamster as the case of the sniffles. Two common reasons hamsters get sick are from baths (NEVER bathe your hamster!), or leaving the cage in a drafty area.

Hamsters with colds should be moved to a warm room and served only soft foods. Instead of water, put lukewarm milk in the hamster's drinking bottle. You can change the milk three times a day for two days.

Hamster Wet Tail

Most commonly associated with the Syrian hamster, this bacterial infection can lead to extreme diarrhea. Caused by stress and an unbalanced diet, you will notice the area around the hamster's anus becomes sticky and wet-looking. He will move in slow motion, will be very quiet and abstain from eating.

Take him to a vet immediately. They will most likely prescribe an antibiotic and a product called "DriTail." Force-feed your hamster liquid vegetables and if he's being really inflexible, add sweetener.

RED URINE

Certain hamster food may cause reddish-color urine. Before jumping to conclusions, change up the hamster food and see if the color returns to normal.

After you determine it is not caused by the food, your hamster may have a urinary tract infection or bladder stones.

Dandelion leaves can be given to your hamster or salt added to his food to encourage urine production and movement of bladder stones. Vitamin C also helps flush out bladder stones.

HAMSTER DIABETES

Hamster diabetes is commonly found in Campbell's hamsters. Diabetes is often hereditary. Some of the symptoms of a hamster with diabetes are: hamster drinking excessively, hamster losing fur on the stomach area and on the hands, excessive urinating. The hamster may also suddenly sleep more than usual or do excessive exercise. Weight loss/gain is also a sign of diabetes.

Remove all sugar from your hamster's diet. This also means eliminating commercially processed foods as well as fresh fruit (which contains fructose). Add more protein and even a Pedialyte solution into the hamster's water bottle.

HAMSTER STROKES

Hamster strokes are not easily identifiable. Strokes often happen during the hamster's waking hours – at night, while you are asleep. You will see the effects of strokes the next morning after the fact.

At times, hamsters experiencing a stroke may tilt their head to one side. Or, he may run around in circles.

Strokes are often caused by old age or overheating. Be sure the hamster's cage is at room temperature between 18°C (65 °F) and 26°C (80°F).

As with humans, a stroke does not necessarily mean the end. Hamsters who have suffered a stroke may live quite a while longer and lead fairly normal lives, although some head tilt may remain.

Note on head tilt: Hamsters may also tilt their heads as a secondary symptom to a respiratory infection. This is caused by the hamster's equilibrium off balance and can easily be treated by antibiotics from the Veterinarian.

HAMSTER SKIN MITES

A skin mite is a small spider-like creature that burrows into the hamster's skin and lives there as a parasite. Your hamster will inevitably be bothered by the intrusion and scratch excessively, possibly causing fur-loss. And thereby, resembling more like your furless-kind.

This condition is a fairly easy fix. Apply an anti-mite spray on a small brush and apply to your hamster two or three times a day. A clean toothbrush or comb works well. Be sure to disinfect the cage and hamster bedding.

HAMSTER EAR MITES

Ear mites, also called Notoedres, live around the hamster's ears but can also invade the hamster's face and feet. Your hamster will itch the infected spots, causing the skin to become crusty. Take your hamster to the vet for special medication in the form of a cream.

HAMSTER CANCERS/TUMORS

If your hamster develops a lump that gets bigger in time, early referral to a vet is vital to increase the chance of successful treatment. The risk of cancer rises as the hamster ages.
Hamster cancers and tumors are often treatable if taken to a vet early.

HAMSTER CYSTS

A cyst is a fluid-filled cavity or sac. Sometimes it contains air or semisolid material. Cysts can become quite large and bothersome. Take your hamster to the vet – they will drain the fluid out of the cyst and get your hamster back on track.

HAMSTER PROTEIN DEFICIENCY - LOSS OF NAILS

A hamster may have some side effects due to lack of proteins in his diet. Side effects include: weak or missing nails, loss of fur, pneumonia, and poor growth (especially in young hamsters).
Be sure you feed your hamster a healthy diet rich in proteins. Peas, beans, soya, and cheese all contain high amounts of protein.

HAMSTER RINGWORM

Hamster ringworm is a type of fungus that grows on the hamster's skin, hairs and nails. As the fungus grows, hairs are broken which then leads to bald areas of the skin.
Hamster ringworm may grow when using plastic enclosed cages since the fungus prefers high humidity.
Always wear gloves when handling a hamster with ringworm. Your vet will provide anti-fungals and explain how to administer.

HAMSTER MOLES

With old age, and we're taking one year old here... moles are quite common. Nothing much to do about those.

3) CLIPPING YOUR HAMSTER'S NAILS AND TEETH

HOW TO CLIP YOUR HAMSTER'S NAILS

Never clip short hamster nails. Only clip your hamster's nails if they start to fold or curl sideways.

To clip your hamster's nails, hold your hamster carefully in a bright light, (where you can more easily see your hamster's translucent nails). Only after he is calm, gently squeeze a toe to separate and extend the nail. Look for a dark interior area. This is the "quick" and you must not cut through it. Place the clipper just beyond the start of the quick and clip his nails one by one.

If you accidentally nick the quick, the nail will bleed. Gently touch the tip with a cotton ball until it stops bleeding.

HOW TO CLIP YOUR HAMSTER'S TEETH

Hamsters' teeth are always growing. To keep them under control, we like to chew on small toys, apple wood, or even dog biscuits. If a hamster has nothing to gnaw on, then our teeth get too long and can puncture our mouth.

The hamster's teeth can be clipped using a pair of nail clippers. Special care must be taken to avoid injuring the hamster's tongue or cheek.

First, hold your hamster by the scruff on his neck, forcing him to "smile" (save us the embarrassment and please do not have a camera ready). Place the nail clippers around the tooth to be cut – only cut .03 cm (1 mm) at a time, never more than that.

4) HIBERNATION

Sudden drops in temperature may lead to hibernation. Ensure your hamster is always in a stable temperature between 18°C (65°F) and 26°C (80°F).

To you, a hibernating hamster will look dead. However, upon closer examination you will see his whiskers oscillate from steady breathing.

If your hamster suddenly goes into hibernation, turn up the heat. You can also place him on a reptile heating pad or covered water bottle (which you should place in the cage so that the hamster won't escape if it recovers) at around 30°C (86°F) for a few hours.

You may also rub the hamster softly. This will encourage him to wake up. Try bottle-feeding your hamster sugared water (one teaspoon of sugar to one cup of water).

When coming out of hibernation, your hamster will shiver – however this is normal and a signal he's feeling better. After he wakes up, give him some soft food (baby food is appropriate) for three days.

SOME ANTIBIOTICS ARE HARMFUL TO HAMSTERS:

- Penicillin
- Ampicillin
- Erythromycin
- Lincomycin
- Vancomycin
- The cephalosporin's

5) FACTS OF LIFE, GETTING OLDER

You don't look a day over 3 Years...

Hamsters have a short life compared to you, furless-giants.

But we all gotta go of something. If it's our time, the most impotents thing you can do for your hamster is to make him as comfortable as possible.

Most hamsters will want to be left alone, however they may need your help if they are unable to get food and water on their own. In which case, offer them morsels of food in front of their face so that they may have access.

Don't try to take your hamster out of the cage. If they are old or dying, they may be too weak to fight it. Simply leave him be in the cage.

6) DEAR, DIARY: MY VERY BAD HAIR DAY

...This morning I woke up on the wrong side of the bedding. My eyes, which usually have a beautiful black sheen, were unusually red and swollen. My ears, which tended to perk up at attention like two straight arrows fell over my forehead like wilted leaves. To top it all off, my furry trusses were matted and greasy.

I examined my complexion in the water bottle...

No, I wouldn't be gracing the cover of "Ham-star" magazine anytime soon. Yuck, I look awful.

I scurried up my hamster tube, made a right after the yellow window, then a left at the blue tunnel where I could perch myself in good standing to observe Stevie's bed.

"ssqqqqqqeakkkk sqqqeakkkkk" I exclaimed. Stevie understands my squeaks and squawks. Most times, he knows I'm just talking to myself – but an urgent "sqqqqqeakkkk sqqqeakkkkk" is never ignored.

I tried again, "sqqqqqeakkkkkk sqqqeaakkkkkk-kahhhhhchooooooooooo!"

Well, that was unexpected.

"Achuuuu achuuuuuu achoooooooooo!"

Stevie appeared, rushing to the blue tube where I perched. My itsy claws clutched the sides of the tunnel walls. He understood immediately.

"Poor Little Fella, you're sick!" Stevie caressed my matted mane, looking concerned.

If there's one thing human beings must know about us hamsters, it's that we don't have bad hair days. I've seen Stevie roll out of bed – his head of hair looks like the end of a mop. For us hamsters, our hair always looks good. We're just blessed with good genes, I guess. And if our hair isn't looking good? We're not feeling good. That's how you know!

Stevie took me to the Animal Doctor, where in my sick delirium I witnessed many beasts. Canines and Felines, Fishes, and Lizards. These creatures looked so strange to me – they come in all shapes and sizes, I can hardly tell if they really exist, or if my fever was causing hallucinations?

Once home, Stevie tucked me into my nest where I remained for three days. My nice human gave me a lot of clean water and fresh food (although I wasn't hungry). He also supplied me three times a day with a peculiar dropper. Something the Animal Doctor gave him.

Stevie held my mouth open and dropped a bit of cherry flavored liquid. I didn't mind the taste. Although, I don't think it was much of a treat. Next time I'm under the weather, I'll ask for another flavor: grape perhaps. Mmmm me like grapes.

[13]

Hamster Breeding

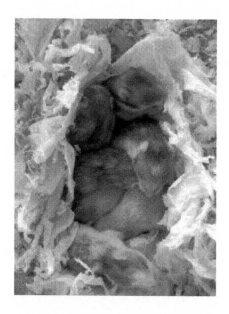

1) RAISING A HAMSTER BROOD

Deciding whether to breed your hamster is a big decision. After all, you are taking on the responsibilities of being a Hamster Grandparent!

Before deciding one way or the other, carefully consider what will be involved. Have a serious discussion with your family to ensure everyone in your household is on board.

Keep in mind that over 5,000,000 homeless animals are euthanized in the United States each year. Why make it <5,000,001 if you are not very serious?

Also, don't expect the finances to follow. You will spend considerable time and money in the enterprise, you really must love it. More importantly, plan ahead. Find homes for the pups in advance.

2) It Takes Two

Female hamsters over the age of 3 weeks go into heat every 4 days for about 12 hours. (Note that they should not be bred before they are 4 weeks old however). Within this 12 hour window every four days, you'll notice particular body language. She will lower her head, and lift her tail – letting you know she's ready to meet the Mister.

After they mate, you will notice a whitish deposit in the vaginal area, and your female will be ready to ditch the male. "Buh-bye, now" – she'll say.

Once pregnant, your female will become aggressive and go hog-wild on the food and water. These are of course healthy behaviors, as she needs to ensure her nest is secure and she is in top form to deliver and care for her young.

Gestation takes between 15 and 18 days for Syrian hamsters, and between 18 and 22 days for Campbells, Chinese, Roborovski, and Winter White hamsters.

After one year of age, your female is ready to become a Grandma and will no longer be genetically fit to rear young.

3) BIRTHING PROCESS AND WHAT NEXT?

The female will likely give birth at night in her nest, when she feels safest. The process will take 10 – 30 minutes. Afterwards, your femme ham will require one week of privacy. Do not handle the pups for at least two weeks; at that time you can gently shift the

babies to clean the cage. By 14 days, the pups will open their eyes and their fur will begin to grow in. After three weeks you will be able to recognize whether they're boys or girls.

This is when it gets particularly fun as the pups can be played with. Observe them as they build their own nests and territories. You're going to need a cage large enough to handle all these little critters!

FINDING A HOME FOR THE PUPS

Of course, you have already found homes for the pups ahead of time but how to go about it?
- Place an ad in the newspaper
- Post notices on bulletin boards at pet shops and feed stores
- Talk to your local school to see if they'd like to adopt a pup for a classroom

And your job through the whole process? Other than securing enough food and safe home for your female and her brood, and finding homes – your job is to butt out. Give her space and be out of her way.

[14]

Websites for Syrian Hamsters

For further resources on Syrians and other pet hamsters, check out the websites on the next page.

INFO:
This book's website is: **<http://www.syrian-hamsters.com>**
It's also a weblog with many news, links, videos and tips!

1) U.K. Relevant Websites

National Hamster Council. Established in 1949, membership includes helpful hamster articles, FAQs, and information on Hamster Shows.

<http://www.hamsters-uk.org/>

Great links, photos, and valuable information managed by two hamster breeders.

<http://www.hamsterama.co.uk/>

Hamster products oriented towards gifts and accessories. Based in the U.K. but ships internationally.

<http://www.hamsters.co.uk/>

Hamster health guides from PSDA vets.

<http://www.pdsa.org.uk/pet-health-advice/syrian-hamsters/>

2) U.S. Relevant Websites

Comprehensive information for hamster fanciers.

<http://www.hamsterland.com>

Connect with other hamster-lovers via the helpful forums and user photos.

<http://www.hamsterhideout.com>

Tips on common hamster issues.

<http://www.hamsterific.com>

The more comic side of hamster ownership. Enjoy products, poetry, and fun links.

<http://www.hamstertours.com>

Index

Black Bear Hamsters 11
Breeders...................................28
bright light..............................20
Campbell Hamster...................11
Chinese Hamster 11, 14
daily diet 53
Dwarf Russian Hamster..........11
exercise wheels........................ 64
female 34
filter..24
fish tanks 44
Golden Hamsters 7, 8
Hamster Ball............................ 64

hamster cages...........................42
heater 24
initial cost 23
lighting....................................24
long-term costs 23
male.. 34
mammals................................. 17
optimum age 35
Roborovski Hamster............... 12
sleep 20, 21, 22, 23, 47, 99
Syrian hamsters7, 9, 10, 13, 14,
    20, 27, 28, 35, 36, 43, 74, 87, 108
Teddy Bear Golden...................11

Photo Credits

PAGE 3:   FROMAC | DREAMSTIME STOCK PHOTOS & STOCK FREE IMAGES

PAGE 5: BY AUGUST GAUL [PUBLIC DOMAIN], VIA WIKIMEDIA COMMONS

PAGE 7: BY ROMAN KLEMENTSCHITZ [PUBLIC DOMAIN], VIA WIKIMEDIA COMMONS

PAGE 9: BY VARDION [PUBLIC DOMAIN], VIA WIKIMEDIA COMMONS

PAGE 11: BY JPBARRASS [PUBLIC DOMAIN], VIA WIKIMEDIA COMMONS

PAGE 13: BY DAIKORAX [PUBLIC DOMAIN], VIA WIKIMEDIA COMMONS

PAGE 14: TRISTANSPOTTER [PUBLIC DOMAIN], VIA WIKIMEDIA COMMONS

PAGE 14: ELEASSAR [PUBLIC DOMAIN], VIA WIKIMEDIA COMMONS

PAGE 15: ASTROGRAPH [PUBLIC DOMAIN], VIA WIKIMEDIA COMMONS

PAGE 16: SY [PUBLIC DOMAIN], VIA WIKIMEDIA COMMONS

PAGE 17: ANONYMOUS [PUBLIC DOMAIN], VIA WIKIMEDIA COMMONS

PAGE 19: ROBOROVSKIHAMSTERS [PUBLIC DOMAIN], VIA WIKIMEDIA COMMONS

PAGE 25: ERIK1980 [PUBLIC DOMAIN], VIA WIKIMEDIA COMMONS

PAGE 32: KAMIL POREMBIŃSKI [PUBLIC DOMAIN], VIA WIKIMEDIA COMMONS

PAGE 41: SHANI870127 [PUBLIC DOMAIN], VIA WIKIMEDIA COMMONS

PAGE 49: BULLET [PUBLIC DOMAIN], VIA WIKIMEDIA COMMONS

PAGE 53: GRANT COCHRANE, VIA FREEDIGITALPHOTOS.NET

PAGE 63: MYLUS [PUBLIC DOMAIN], VIA WIKIMEDIA COMMONS

PAGE 65: WILL 210 [PUBLIC DOMAIN], VIA WIKIMEDIA COMMONS

PAGE 67: DACOOKIEMAN | DREAMSTIME STOCK PHOTOS & STOCK FREE IMAGES

PAGE 73: JAMES BARKER | DREAMSTIME STOCK PHOTOS & STOCK FREE IMAGES

PAGE 83: ANDRIY.BABETS [PUBLIC DOMAIN], VIA WIKIMEDIA COMMONS

PAGE 93: KAMIL POREMBIŃSKI [PUBLIC DOMAIN], VIA WIKIMEDIA COMMONS

PAGE 97: BLOTTY | <u>DREAMSTIME STOCK PHOTOS</u> & <u>STOCK FREE IMAGES</u>

PAGE 107: MASTAWINDU [PUBLIC DOMAIN], VIA WIKIMEDIA COMMONS

PAGE 109: DACOOKIEMAN | <u>DREAMSTIME STOCK PHOTOS</u> & <u>STOCK FREE IMAGES</u>

PAGE 111: JAMES BARKER <u>DREAMSTIME STOCK PHOTOS</u> & <u>STOCK FREE IMAGES</u>

ABOUT THE PUBLISHER

"Karola Brecht is a publisher and writer living and working in Heidelberg, Germany. Miss Brecht is born and raised on a farm. When she's not reminiscing about her special friendships with Twinkle Toes, Emir and Blinky, she is working at a veterinary practice. She enjoys working with animals, especially with pets. If you want to leave her a message, please contact her at:

www.storie-di-karola.com

karola.brecht@storie-di-karola.com

She is happy about any message!

Made in the USA
San Bernardino, CA
10 December 2017